Waldorf Journal Projects #10 and #11
April – May 2008
Waldorf Publications

Morality and Ethics in Education

Compiled and edited by
David Mitchell

Printed with support from the Waldorf Curriculum Fund

Published by:

Waldorf Publications
at the Research Institute for Waldorf Education
38 Main Street
Chatham, NY 12037

Waldorf Journal Projects #10–11
Title: *Morality and Ethics in Education*
Translators: Karin DiGiacomo, John McAlice, René Querido, Jan-Kees Saltet, Ted Warren
Editor: David Mitchell
Proofreader: Ann Erwin

© 2014 by Waldorf Publications
ISBN # 978-1-936367-62-7
originally published in 2008 as two separate Waldorf Journal Projects, #10 and #11

Gratitude is expressed to the editors of Steinerskolen and the individual authors for granting permissions to translate the essays for North America.

Contents

Foreword 5

Journal Project #10

Education and the Moral Life 7
  Rudolf Steiner

Education of the Will as the Wellspring of Morality 10
  Michaela Glöckler

Human Development and the Forces of Morality 19
  Ernst-Michael Kranich

Conscience and Morality 33
  Karl Brodersen

The West and East in Us 44
  Jørgen Smit

Reincarnation and Pedagogy 50
  Valentin Wember

Moral Imagination 58
  Oscar Borgman Hansen

The Christmas Mystery and the Knowledge of Evil 63
  Hermann Poppelbaum

Evil and the Well-Intended 67
  Oscar Borgman Hansen

Craft and Morality 72
  Thomas Weihs

Journal Project #11

Forces Leading to Health and Illness in Education 81
   Rudolf Steiner

*Transformative Education and the Right to an
Inviolate Childhood*..................................... 91
   Christopher Clouder

The Human Self 101
   Karl Brodersen

The Free and the Unfree Spirit 104
   Ted Warren

Recapitulation (Recall) in the High School Main Lessons 108
   Ken Power

The Odyssey of Conscience *by Henning Andersen*.............. 111
   reviewed by Oddvar Granly

War and Peace and Moral Imagination....................... 122
   Oskar Borgman Hansen

The Power of Moral Education—Geography 126
   Christof Goepfer

Ethics and the Perspective on Nature 133
   Oskar Borgman Hansen

The Being of the Internet 140
   Sergei Prokofieff

Foreword

The Waldorf Journal Project, sponsored by the Waldorf Curriculum Fund, brings translations of essays, magazine articles, and specialized studies from around the world to English-speaking audiences. This edition of translations from journals in Norway, Germany, and Switzerland is comprised of articles intended for personal and faculty study.

The theme for this double edition, Journal Projects #10 and #11, is morality and ethics in education. At a conference at Harvard University exploring the needs of education in the 21st century, a group of experts called for a return of morality and ethics to curricula of the American schools. It was mentioned that Waldorf education has successfully incorporated these themes and a question arose: Why don't they share their ideas? Waldorf Journals are an attempt to do just that. There is much written on these topics, and this is merely a sampling.

The first article is by Rudolf Steiner in which he sets the moral and ethical aims of Waldorf education. This is followed by an article by Dr. Michaela Glöckler on educating the will as the font of awakened morality. Ernst-Michael Kranich follows with a scholarly treatise. Then comes Norwegian Waldorf teacher Karl Brodersen with a short but poignant article on conscience and morality and how early philosophers viewed them. His former colleague Jørgen Smit speaks next, directly to the teacher on self-development and illustrates specific qualities of Eastern and Western thinking and morality. Valentin Wember explores reincarnation, and Oscar Hansen examines moral imagination, motives for social action, moral technique, and the role of art in education. The concept of evil is developed between Hermann Poppelbaum and Oscar Hansen. Journal #10 concludes with a magnificent piece by Dr. Thomas Weihs on craft and morality.

Journal #11 starts with another article by Rudolf Steiner; in it he sets forth the basis of lifelong health upon the foundation of a moral and ethical education. This is followed by an article by Christopher Clouder in which he makes a case for the protection of childhood. Karl Brodersen looks at the nature and development of the moral "self" in each child: How do we change during our lives but remain the same? How do we take responsibility for our actions? Edward Warren explores the free and unfree spirit of the adolescent. Oddvar Granby reviews Henning Andersen's book *The Odyssey of Conscience*, and Oskar Hansen explores war and peace from a moral perspective. Next we take a practical look at geography in an essay by Christof Goepfer who shows how a school can provide moral development. This is followed by Oskar Hansen's thoughts on the abyss created by modern science and morality. We end with a provocative article by Sergei Prokofieff on the being of the Internet.

    We hope that you will be both informed and inspired by these writings. All the articles are available on-line at
http://www.waldorflibrary.org

    For those not interested in downloading the material, inexpensive spiral-bound copies are available from:
Waldorf Publications
458 Harold Meyers Road
Earlton, NY 12058

Education and the Moral Life

by

Rudolf Steiner

The tasks of the teacher and educator culminate in what he is able to achieve for the moral strength and bearing of the young folk entrusted to him. In elementary school education, he will find himself confronted with great difficulties in this matter. One difficulty is that the moral teaching must permeate all he does for his pupils. The orientation of all the teaching and educational work in a moral sense can attain far more than special or separate instruction in morals. This however is paramountly a matter of educational tact. For indeed, crude "moralizings" in every conceivable connection—impressive though they may be, made in the moment when they are brought forward—do not in the long run bring about the result that is intended. Another difficulty is this: The child, when entering the "elementary" school, has the basic moral tendencies of life already developed.

Until the period at about the seventh year when he undergoes the change of teeth, the child lives fully given up to his surroundings. The child is, as one might say, altogether "sense." As the eye lives in colors, so does the whole child live in the expressions of the life of his environment. Every gesture, every movement of the father or the mother is accompanied by an answering experience throughout the inner organism of the child. Until this time the brain, the whole of human nature, is being formed and molded. And from the brain there goes out, in this first epoch of life, all which gives the organism its inner stamp and character. All that takes place in the environment—all manifestation of life—is imitated in the finest manner in the brain. The young child's learning to speak depends entirely on this.

But it is not only the external features in the behavior of the environment which are echoed in the nature of the child and which set their stamp upon its inner character. It is the content of soul, the moral content, too. A father who reveals himself before the child in expressions of life that arise from a quick, hot-tempered nature will cause the child to take on—even to the most delicate organic structures of the tissues—the tendency to the gesture-like expression of quick temper. A mother behaving in a timid, frightened way implants in the child organic structures and tendencies of movement, such that the body becomes an instrument which the soul will then want to use in the sense of fear and of timidity.

In the period of the change of teeth, the child possesses a bodily organism which will react in a very definite way, spiritually and morally, to all that is of the soul. In this condition—with an organism of definite tendency and inclination as regards the moral things—the elementary school teacher and educator receives the child. If the teacher does not clearly see this fact, he will be in danger of approaching the child with moral impulses which the child will unconsciously reject because he has, in the constitution of his own body, the hindrances to their acceptance.

The essential thing, however, is this. It is true that the child, when entering the elementary school, already has the fundamental inclinations acquired by imitation of his environment. But by a right treatment these can be transformed. A child who has grown up in a hot-tempered environment has received from it his organic stamp and form. This must not be left unnoticed; it requires to be reckoned with and it can be changed. In the second period of life—from the change of teeth to puberty—we can, if we really reckon with it, so change and form it that it gives the soul the foundation for a quick and ready presence of mind, bold and courageous action in cases in life when this is necessary. In like manner a child-organization resulting from an anxious, timid environment can provide the basis for the development of a fine sense of modesty and chastity. Thus, a true knowledge of the nature of man is the basic need in moral education.

But the teacher and educator must have a clear perception of what it is that child nature in general requires for its development between the change of teeth and puberty. (These requirements have been described by me in the *Education Course,* reproduced by Albert Steffen in the *Goetheanum Weekly,* and now available in book form.) In effect we can bring about the transformation of the basic moral tendencies, and also the further development of those which we must regard as right and good, only by directing our efforts to the life of feeling, the moral sympathies and antipathies. Nor is it abstract maxims and ideas, but pictures which work upon the life of feeling. In our teaching work we have everywhere the opportunity to place before the soul of the child pictures of human (and, in parable, of supra-human) life and conduct, pictures by which the moral sympathies and antipathies may be awakened. It is the feeling judgment upon moral matters which should be developed in the time between the change of teeth and puberty.

As the child before the change of teeth gives himself up, imitatively, to the immediate expressions of the life of his environment, so in the time from the change of teeth until puberty he is devoted to the authority of what the teacher and educator says. The human being cannot awaken in later life to the right use of his moral freedom if in this second period of life he was unable to unfold himself with full devotion to the natural and accepted authority of those who educated him. True as this is for all education and all teaching, it is true most especially for what is moral. By and through the educator whom he respects and honors, the child sees feelingly what is good and what is evil. The educator represents the Order of the Universe. It is through the grown-up human being that the evolving human being first must learn to know the World.

We can observe what an important educational impulse this involves when, with a true knowledge of the human being, we have to find our right relation to the child after the first third of the second period of life, say between the ninth and tenth birthday. Here a most important point in life is reached. We note how half-unconsciously, with a more or less dim feeling, the child is going through something that means very much to him. On our meeting the child in the right way at this juncture, untold things will depend for the whole of his later life. To express consciously what the child now experiences in dream-like feeling, we should have to say: There comes before the child's soul the question, "Whence has the teacher the power which I, believing in him with such reverence, accept?" To the unconscious depths of the child's soul, the educator must prove that he has this authority rightly, in that he is firmly grounded in the Order of the World. By a true knowledge of the human being we shall find, at this point of time, how one child will require but a few words rightly spoken and another many. But something decisive must happen at this point, and only the nature of the child himself can teach us what it has to be. Things of untold importance may be achieved by the educator just at this point in life for the moral power, the moral certainty, and moral bearing of the child.

If the moral feeling-judgment is well developed when puberty arrives, it can then in the next period of life be taken into the free will. The adolescent leaving elementary school will take with him into life, from the aftereffects of the school years, in his soul the feeling that the moral impulses are unfolding in him in social life and in intercourse with his fellow men out of the inner power of his human nature. And the result after puberty will be a moral strength of the will, which until then was germinating in the rightly cultivated moral feeling-judgment.

Education of the Will as the Wellspring of Morality

by

Michaela Glöckler

translated by Jan-Kees Saltet

This article is a written adaptation of a lecture by Michaela Glöckler of July 6, 1993, which was printed in the *Erziehungskunst #10* of October 1993. The preface is part of the introduction which was written by the editors of *Erziehungskunst*.

In the face of increasing violence and aggression, the question becomes more and more pressing: How can education contribute to the moral development of children and adolescents? The usual approach to the problem often assumes that one has only to explain the rules of social behavior to children and that better insight will automatically lead to an improvement of behavior. Experience shows, however, that one doesn't reach the source of behavior in this way. Intellectual moralizing or giving reprimands does not deeply affect the way children act. The sources of moral or "immoral" action reside in that unconscious layer of the soul in which the will impulses originate. Therefore, Michaela Glöckler asks: What really reaches this sphere at the different stages of child development? How does the education of the will create the conditions from which morality proper can develop when the child comes of age?

When we talk about education of the will, the question immediately arises if the will can be educated at all, because we look upon the will as something that belongs uniquely to ourselves. We feel it is our private domain in which we want to be sovereign, increasingly so the more we become able to assess our own position in life. Our hackles go up as soon as we feel interference in this personal realm, or, as it was called in the 1960s at the time of the student revolutions, we feel "manipulated." Manipulation of the will was the catchword that kindled the emancipation movement for spiritual liberation of the students.

One can ask the question posed above at an even more fundamental level: does education always have to be interference? Or could one think of an education in which one takes over the responsibility until the child comes of age, taking the place of the child, as it were, until the reins can be passed on? After all, full maturity and responsibility are goals that we reach only, "if we're honest about it," between age twenty and thirty.

In the deliberations below, we shall connect the question regarding an education without manipulation to another question: How do we reach the will of the child at all and motivate the child or adolescent, taking into account the different stages of development? I would like to understand the will here not as vacillating deliberations and vague feelings with regard to possible courses of action, but as the impulse to carry out what we are actually able to achieve. Will results in activity; and when we do nothing, our will is actually not functioning at that moment.

Willed action, however, comprises not only physical actions such as moving tables, setting up house, pursuing a professional craft, handling machines, and so forth. It also means being engaged, body and soul, in thoughts and feelings. Of course we can also think without conscious engagement of the will and give ourselves over to associations as in daydreaming, where we do not employ our will power and surrender to whatever wells up from within. In our feeling life this corresponds to abandoning ourselves to our emotions and reacting spontaneously to any stimulus. We do, however, have the option to engage our will consciously and, for example, digest the feeling, replace it with another one, or even choose not to react. Whoever has tried knows that it isn't always easy to exercise influence on feelings and thoughts by dint of the will. We meet this phenomenon also in the sphere of our actions. Even when we are under the impression that we exert conscious control over our actions, we are capable of doing things which in retrospect we have to judge differently and come to the realization: I didn't really want to do that, that wasn't I; I have acted without proper involvement of my ego. In other words, we can think, feel, and also act in such a way that our waking ego doesn't actually take part. I would like to go on now to explore the stages of the education of the will and the way children and adolescents can be motivated. This will be based on the premise that the aim is not to promote the exercise of the will without ego or to live out impulsive actions arising out of the body. Instead, the education of children and adolescents should require that I be responsible to the personality at every step of the educational process, always bearing in mind what is age appropriate for the student in my care. Thereby I would like "education of the will" to be understood as something which one could designate as the willingness of the human being to act spiritually, emotionally, and physically in proper relationship to the ego, to the person.

Education of the Will in the Early Years

When we observe the developmental phases of the child, we discover characteristic learning dispositions and corresponding ways for education to work on the will. At preschool age, in the so-called phase of sensory-motor intelligence, the child's motor system is closely linked to the visual impressions and to all other sensory stimuli. One reaches the will of the child (i.e., her movement organism) and mobilizes her willingness to act by way of the surrounding sense impressions, by giving her examples to imitate which causes her to exercise her will. Even though the child orients herself so readily to examples and spontaneously engages her will in that way, everything still has to be learned, so there is always a certain threshold to be conquered. It is most impressive to witness this conquering of a threshold when children learn to walk, which, all in all, takes about a year until the first small steps really succeed and become more certain. Learning from examples even goes so far that children imitate all kinds of peculiar characteristics of the gaits of adults around them. It shouldn't be underestimated how much exertion of the will and effort is needed to achieve all this early in life. This goes to show that the education of the will is identical with learning, with building up the ability to learn, and we see the same principle at work when we proceed to other levels. Education of the will on a physical level has to do with dexterity and coordination; it means developing integrated, well-adapted motor skills. Correspondingly, moving to the level of soul and spirit, education of the will means building up a maximum ability to handle emotional and mental processes. Thus one can say that there is no learning process resulting in a skill we can use later on which is not the result of an effort of will. All capacities we have at our disposal as adults have been gained by exerting ourselves earlier on.

We can add a further experience when we ask the question: What prompts children to imitate most readily? For example, when a child talks back and doesn't want to follow, what induces her immediately to change her mind and comply, even though she just protested? When this child notices that the adult has something really important in mind and is deeply interested in pursuing that, all protest will vanish into the background. When the adult fully identifies with whatever she is engaged, she creates the best conditions for the child to enter into her intention. The child absorbs that through her senses and will attempt to imitate it. That way she makes it into her own movement, her own activity and her own dexterity.

Motivation of the Will during the Elementary School Years

The phase characterized above, during which it is enough for the adult to be involved in order to motivate and enthuse the child, lasts until the eighth or ninth year at most. If the mode of learning described above would remain the same, we wouldn't encounter the many educational challenges that occur from here on until puberty. At the beginning of elementary school, children can no longer be motivated directly by just giving an example. The demands of the motor system begin to take second-place and it becomes possible for children to sit still for longer periods of time. Then begins a phase when the will can be mobilized only when children like something. That occurs because during this developmental phase, the will is no longer directed by the sense impressions but by the feelings. The best incentive now comes from the teacher who is fully engaged in what she says or deems right to such a degree that her own enthusiasm and deeply-felt conviction set the feelings of the child in motion. For example, the teacher will have succeeded in speaking about Caesar if a pupil comes home every day and feels inspired to recount to his mother the latest about Caesar, because he's so completely engaged by the subject. A few days later, he comes home, throws his backpack in a corner, and runs up to his room past the open kitchen door where his mother is waiting for the next installment about Caesar. All he can utter is, "Mom, Caesar is dead!" Deeply moved, he throws himself onto the bed and can hardly deal with Caesar's assassination. It doesn't matter if a sixth grader knows exactly when Caesar was born and died, or when the battles were. What has an educational effect at this age is what moves the will through the feelings, such as the digestion of strong feelings of sadness and indignation illustrated by this example.

Insight as a Motivator of the Will of the Adolescent

At the end of the elementary school years, or at the latest the beginning of high school, the teacher notices that biographies don't reach the pupils in the same way. At the onset of puberty, teenagers can no longer be motivated primarily through their feelings. Youngsters are much more likely to become motivated when they are able to act out of understanding. Without thought or insight adolescents don't feel motivated. They will sometimes even opt not to do things they actually like when they don't see the sense of doing them. A toddler overcomes her dislike of learning when she has an example she loves. A grade-school child overcomes a lack of engagement when she experiences strong interest and understanding in an adult, which have the effect of enthusing her and mobilizing her will. An adolescent needs a grown-up who is full of questions, who is striving for understanding and teaches the pupils out of this quest.

When the students sense this search in a teacher, they can relate. Teachers who embody this ideal tend to be most beloved. When the high school teacher brings the material in such a way that she gives the facts but leaves the act of will, which is necessary to gain insight, to the pupils themselves, the capacities of will are being awakened on a spiritual level. To illustrate this, I would like to describe an example from a physiology block in tenth grade, in which we had just discussed the circulation of the blood in the human being.

I had told the students about the discovery of the closed circulatory system by William Harvey. In Harvey's day, people thought that the blood was built up by the nutritional processes in the center of the body and was used up in the periphery. It wasn't yet known that the blood returns to the heart, but it was known through dissection that the heart is astonishingly small and can hold only about 70 ml of blood. By feeling the pulse, it had been observed that the heart typically beats about 80 times per minute. Having learned this, the class began to make up the craziest theories about how Harvey had come to see that the blood must circulate in a closed system. Finally one pupil reasoned as follows: When the heart passes on 70 ml of blood with every pulse, 80 times per minute, the total volume of blood of 5.6 liters has to pass through the heart every minute. If one calculates the volume per hour and then multiplies that by 24, the total amount of blood circulating in a day is thousands of liters. Since no human being can eat or drink as much as would be necessary to produce such a huge quantity of blood, the student concluded that the blood must return to the center.

The pupil who was able to develop this logical train of thought was not one of the most capable students and had not actively involved himself in class up to that point. It was an archetypal pedagogical situation when I witnessed how the whole class participated in the boy's happiness at having found the right solution, and everyone shared his triumph because it had been prepared by all of them, each pupil having wrestled with this problem. Coming to such an individual insight can make an adolescent into a different person because he feels a direct connection to his will, having mastered the problem by his own efforts. This results in increased self-confidence and a feeling of being able to think independently. This triumphal feeling can last for weeks, and the teacher can use it by keeping this confidence alive.

How Education of the Will Builds Self-confidence and Becomes a Wellspring of Morality

We now come to the essence of what it means to educate the will. We must offer the children age-appropriate materials in such a way that they are induced to become active themselves. All that happens in school, be it examples, stories, or other pedagogical stimuli, should, in the last analysis, serve to bring out independent activity. Learning to walk is something you have to do yourself, digesting feelings is something you have to learn yourself, and grasping things intellectually is something you have to accomplish yourself, no matter if others have understood the same things before you. It would mean nothing for your own development if things were taken in purely as information. Seen this way, education of the will means always awakening the pupil's own activity and therefore is the most important process for building self-confidence.

When you're clumsy, you feel uncertain inside your body. When you have no self control, you will lack confidence in your interactions with other people. Inasmuch as the will has been addressed and exercised at different levels during education, self-confidence will be anchored in corresponding levels of body, soul, and spirit. Thus the education of the will in children and teenagers should have as its main aim the strengthening of self-confidence.

Many people today are extremely self-conscious; they tend to be highly awake, sensitive, and vulnerable. At the same time they suffer from an enormous lack of inner conviction and self-confidence, which can often be traced back to a development of the intellectual capacities which has taken place without a corresponding development of the will. This raises the question: How can the education of the will become a source of morality? For it is so that a human being who is out of touch with herself and therefore has no self-confidence will have no access to the sources of her own morality. When we say morality "in whatever way we would like to define the term" we mean in the last analysis: dependability, reliability and the capacity to become interested, without which it is impossible to relate to anything or anyone. Connecting in a moral way essentially means connecting inwardly, and without involvement of the ego a moral bond is impossible among people. When a healthy relationship to our own inner being has not been established by building up a healthy self-confidence, we have no access to the wellspring of morality.

In present-day social circumstances, the will threatens to derail more and more in the form of aggression and violence. Violence and extremism are the results of a failed development of the will, for a successful education of the will leads to a strong, dependable relationship to the world. On a physical level the child learns dexterity by handling and mastering the things of the world, and in so doing learns to relate to the earth. Later children learn to get involved on a soul level by feeling empathy and compassion, they establish a relationship to the world with their hearts, and finally, as their powers of comprehension ripen, with their heads. Inhuman actions can arise only in situations where the human being cannot establish a relationship.

Obstacles to the Education of the Will

An education of the will is being thwarted because we unwittingly do things which prevent children from developing the right things at the right time, for instance, by furthering the motor system in the early years and the capacity to feel and think later on. Young children are deprived of movement. We drive them everywhere, we give them few opportunities to exercise their limbs, and we set them in front of the television, where they sit still. Maybe it is not our intention, but in doing so we practice an education in which the ego is constantly being forced to detach from the will. By forcing the ego thus to detach from the will in the motor system, the processes of growth and development at this age are taking place for hours on end without participation of the ego. As a result there will be an increased tendency to act without participation of the ego, and this tendency arises directly out of the physical constitution, it is body-bound.

During the elementary school phase we likewise encounter obstacles which stand in the way of entering into things with the feelings. This will especially be the case when the education is inartistic, one-sidedly intellectual, or oriented too much toward passing on information. All too often the pupils experience how teachers will be almost apologetic, explaining to them that they also find the material boring and uninteresting but are forced to pass it on to the students. Therefore everything the teacher brings to the young pupils must be something in which she is deeply interested. Nothing lames the development of the will in the second phase more than critical aloofness, intellectualism, and the abstract passing on of information, which breeds in the pupils a mocking, distant attitude towards the world.

The third type of obstacle, which we see especially in high school, is a certain type of uncertainty on a spiritual level. In that type of thinking everything is possible, nothing seems binding anymore, and there is no real responsibility to the truth. Pragmatism prevails; the question is no longer whether a thing is true, but whether it is doable. This touches on a central problem facing scientists today.

Present-day culture directly forces our children and youth to bail out "in body, soul, and spirit." The ego is no longer given a chance to become interested and is in essence barred from establishing a meaningful relationship to the world; therefore we have to resign ourselves to existing circumstances which are no longer accessible to our will.

A few years ago an article appeared in the German magazine *Spiegel* about a new kindergarten in Hamburg which specialized in children of drug addicts. There it was found that three things can counteract possible addiction in the children. The first requirement is to free the mind of any prejudice when talking to the child and to show absolute interest in everything she brings. With this should go openness and acceptance. In our hearts, we should carry an attitude which gives a child the feeling, "You are just right; I like you just the way you are." Thirdly, it is important to give the child, once a day at least, a clear sense of achievement: "You did it!" It was found that children thrive in these circumstances, regardless of educational content they receive besides, and, *Spiegel* reports optimistically, the children won't be tempted to grab the needles lying around at home. Thus one may actually trust that these dangers can largely be avoided when an interest in the world has been awakened and a can-do attitude has been fostered.

From Education to Self-education

Even with a successful education of the will, things can go wrong, either in youth or later in life. Something can throw a wrench in the works and everything will be brought into question. Even with the fruits of a good education and all the necessary prerequisites, the human being repeatedly comes to stand in front of an abyss and must ask: Do I have the will or not? Thus we come to realize that the best education of the world doesn't release us from a constant daily effort to transform education into self-education; it is part of being human.

This brings us to a large problem for present-day society, because our culture provides little incentive to take our own inner development in hand. Recently, I have met many people who told me with regard to the atrocities perpetrated in Yugoslavia: "I have come to the limits of my comprehension. I cannot stand this any longer. It is impossible for me to come to terms with this." This shows how hard it is today, especially for young people, to be exposed to the inhumanity in the world without sliding into a state of despair about existence as a whole. This challenge often deprives people of their vitality. We can thus see a trend in modern historical development that challenges us to come to a real inner decision: Do I have the will to devote myself wholeheartedly to bringing more true humanity into the world? Morality is always a question of decision and commitment. Even with a very good education I can still behave very badly at times when I have made wrong decisions.

The source of morality becomes a living experience only when we begin to make decisions without the involvement of parents or teachers. Even when students willingly accept things that have been decided for them, sooner or later in life they will notice that certain decisions have to be made anew at some point, this time independently. This shows that education of the will alone, while giving access to the source of morality, isn't enough to unlock this source. Only the free human ego can do this by a conscious decision to live and work in a way that is a worthy of true humanity. Therefore morality can mean no less than an ongoing, lifelong struggle to participate honestly and lovingly in the evolution of humanity and the individual, both at home and at work.

Acting Out of Love and Freedom

We now come to the most delicate point of this theme—to the point where we as individuals must confront ourselves, where we discover our limits and realize the extent of our powers of will, compassion, and insight. Here we must face the questions: With the possibilities at my disposal, how do I find the strength to do something constructive for the progress of those around me and for the world as a whole? Where are the ideas and the ideals that give me moral orientation? If, at that point, I cannot wholeheartedly say yes to the course of action I decide for myself, it won't be a true moral action. It may be something good which serves others, a useful action at best, but it will be a moral action only when I do it with the full involvement of my ego, when it is an expression of my being. That means when I love what I do and act out of free choice.

As far as the source of morality is concerned, freedom and love are identical concepts. Thus we can feel truly motivated for our actions only when we can retain our individual integrity, when we know why we do something. We are moral in our feelings when we can meet others and ourselves with interest and know where we stand. We come to a moral relationship to the world in our thinking when our quest for knowledge is directed towards truths and honesty.

We can grasp the ego as source of our personality in a threefold way. We can experience it as ego consciousness, which gives us the sense of a unified being. On the one hand, we experience it as the strength of self-confidence, on the other as consciousness or center, as I. As soon as we employ the ego, we do so on the level of thinking, feeling, and willing. Therefore this ego manifests in a threefold way: as love for truth, as love for our fellow human beings and the world, and as the striving for autonomy and freedom. These qualities are constantly being threatened by the fact that we are tempted to be dishonest and loveless.

We see that the ego lives between the ideal and a counter-ideal. The ego holds the middle between the longing for truth and mendacity, between the capacities of love and hatred, between the striving for freedom and the lust for power. This source of morality is constantly endangered from within by our lower ego, which always threatens the higher ego. It is only possible for us to conceptualize this higher ego in the form of ideals and we can only, so to speak, pull it down into ourselves. If, however, we didn't have the lower ego, which always wants to hinder us from rising above ourselves and conquering our egotism, we would not be able to be moral beings. Animals have no choice but to act according to the behavioral patterns of their species; only human beings can act immorally. We are not complete at birth, and our physical, psychological and spiritual constitution doesn't keep itself in balance. As we grow older we become aware of the necessity of self-education. This involves acceptance of the way we are and a free resolve to act in the world according to our gifts and capacities. In contrast to the animals, we are always evolving, working to realize our potential. Because of this, human beings are capable of immoral deeds; we can make mistakes and stray from the path. A successful education of the will is therefore a good preparation for a second birth later in life, when we take our education into our own hands. Such a step is a sign of healthy self-confidence and self-knowledge. What a feat to break through to the source of morality, to become truly self-reliant, to become one's self! When we succeed, it is indeed a most infectious thing for those around to witness. Schools today must therefore be places where people can experience how infectious health is!

Michaela Glöckler, M.D., has been active as a pediatrician and school doctor for many years. She is the author of numerous articles and several books on children's health and Waldorf education, including A Guide to Child Health, *published by Floris Books. Since 1988 she has directed the Medical Section at the Goetheanum in Dornach, Switzerland. She lectures widely throughout the world on behalf of the Waldorf movement and is an active partner in the Alliance for Childhood.*

Human Development and the Forces of Morality

An Anthropology of Moral Education

by

Ernst-Michael Kranich

translated by Jon McAlice

Among the notes and fragments of the German poet Novalis we find the following remark: "Rightly understood, morality is the actual realm of life for a human being."[1] What we call morality begins when we look beyond our narrow personal wishes and interests; when we free ourselves of the bias of egotism; and when other people, other beings become important to us and we feel the urge to share their experiences. When empathy and caring move us to dedicate our lives to others, to place ourselves at the service of our fellow human beings and our surroundings, then the realm in which we live can be called moral. It is easy to imagine that life in this realm can grow ever stronger and more powerful. As this happens, we move from having a childlike dependency on our environment to taking on a co-creative role. We can experience how our actions flow from a living center, our own "I" or ego.[2] Through this living center we are able to gain insight into the nature of things, to see the spiritual in outer manifestations. In this living center, this ego, we experience the inspirations of our artistic creativity. We can sense that human nature reaches its highest form of expression when we connect ourselves with our surroundings through moral forces and impulses. When this occurs, the illusion of separation disappears. The moral realm is clearly related to the element of warmth, as well, which, with its invigorating force, penetrates the surface and reaches deep within.

Morality is the realm of human perfection. It can be attained only gradually. Here lies the future of humanity, an endangered future. If we want to follow up on these introductory remarks and work toward a more concrete understanding, we must begin by posing a series of questions:

- What is the origin of moral impulses?
- What are the stages of soul development that enable it to bring moral impulses to life?
- What are the outer conditions—the configurations of the human body—that make possible the realization of moral impulses?
- In what ways is a developing individual connected to the various forces of morality?

Anatomical Basis of Morality

If the human body were a structure that was completely determined by the laws of heredity, it would be impossible to understand how it could become an instrument through which a self is able to realize moral impulses in action. The impersonal nature of genetic determination would lead to a body that was complete unto itself. How could it possibly become the tool of ethical or moral action? This is only possible in that the ego plays a role in the formation of the body.

In early childhood and, especially, in the first year of life, the individual, through her own effort, gradually takes hold of the body from within, working to permeate it from top to bottom with the forces of her will. When a child stands, we can recognize in the vertical posture an inner being, who through an act of will overcomes gravity and holds herself in balance. Self-balanced uprightness is a sign of centeredness. A self arises in a being that acts intentionally and experiences itself as centered.

As a child's self grasps its body and raises it up against the forces of gravity, it works to re-form the body. I have presented this in depth in other writings and wish only to call certain details to mind.[3] The legs of a small child tend to bow outward. The weight of the body presses down on them. By the time a child has reached age seven, a characteristic human posture has been attained: feet and ankles are close together, and thighs slant outward above the knees and carry the weight of the body in the hip joints. This new structural configuration, with its narrow base and sovereign support of the body, brings a quality of centeredness and inner activity to expression. The form of the legs takes on the signature of active selfhood. Feet elongate. An arch is formed through the activity of walking, a powerful impulse of movement in the foot. The weight of the body is overcome through an inner concentration of forces. This is why we can find a point of balance between the ball and the heel of the foot. Thanks to the formation of the arch, the foot receives the signature of the activity of the ego and becomes the foundation for the free posture of the human body. [4]

The skeletal-muscular system within our trunk also goes through a process of transformation. In striving to raise the head in order to look at the world around it, a child forms the upward curvature of the neck, the cervical lordosis. In striving to stand upright and to carry the body freely, a child forms the downward curve toward the base of the spine, the lumbar lordosis.

When we follow these transformations physiologically, we discover something significant: The ego of a child is at work in the unconscious depths of the body, where the bones are formed and the muscles develop. Through this work the ego impresses its signature on the child's body. The ego forms the body to fit, in that it brings itself to expression. In the course of the process, the form of the knee joint and the arrangement of the tendons develop in such a way that when the leg is completely extended, the thigh and the lower leg are pressed together in what is functionally a single structure. Similarly, in a fully upright posture, the head of the femur is pressed so firmly into the cuplike acetabulum of the hipbone that a functional unity of the two is ensured. A human becomes a being who, when standing, rests completely in the body's static equilibrium. In standing, he enters a state of will-permeated rest. All the tendencies to movement and states of tension that vibrate in an animal's body even when at rest are eradicated. Thus, in early childhood, a human becomes a being that, even in the form of the body, brings to expression a tendency to move not simply impulsively, but rather out of peaceful centeredness to form inner goals and then to realize them in action. Thanks to a body's restfulness, the will organization of a human being is open to intentions which the individual forms within, in the thinking selfhood.

As this transformative process takes place in a child's bodily structure, a similar process takes place in the brain. Those sections of the brain, thanks to which an individual is able to grasp conceptually what he perceives, are more finely developed. This occurs primarily in the period up to age three. The formally highest areas are developed in the frontal part of the brain, just behind the forehead. By the time a child is six, the structures here will have developed that allow him to grasp complicated relationships, the basis for intentional action. The frontal cortex is also the basis for the recognition of creativity, which gives action its meaning. It enables us to work through our experience and practice self-reflection. Clinical observations show that the development of the frontal cortex allows us to grasp ideas that raise us above fleeting impressions and desires to a recognition of the tasks and necessities of life. When such ideas become the basis for action, human life begins to become the expression of morality. Both the will-organization of the skeletal-muscular system and the physical basis for thinking take on a configuration in which the self can bring itself to expression. The thinking through which a person conceives intentional actions is permeated with the power and prudence of selfhood. This configuration forms bodily conditions for the realization of moral impulses in our outer life.

This configuration is also the basis for the development of certain moral traits. By the time she is seven, a child is able to recall in inner pictures what she experiences in her surroundings. These pictures are not rigid, as are most objects, but flexible. Thus the child can let the pictures flow into one another and, in passing from one to the other, recognize relationships. In doing so she exercises her thinking in the medium of pictorial images.

Virtues

What happens in a human being when thoughts immerse themselves in will? A person decides to speak the truth in a given situation although he knows that, from an opportunistic point of view, it would be better to say nothing or to say something else. When he raises this decision to the level of a will impulse and stands for the truth, then we say he is upright or honorable. If a person resolves not to take more than he needs to sustain his existence, and then lives up to his resolution, we say he is modest. And when he fulfills an agreement, we call his behavior reliable.

Such thoughts affect the will not only case-by-case; they may become such an integral part of the will that they form a character trait. Thought and will reach a state of harmony in which, as in the resonance of two notes sounded together, something new is created. In this case, a person is not simply upright in this or that situation, uprightness becomes something that grows in him. He is not just now and again modest; rather modesty comes to life within him. The same is true for reliability. When selfless goals of action connect themselves so deeply with the will that this takes on a stable orientation, virtues such as justice, loyalty, carefulness, responsibility, helpfulness, courage, deliberation, uprightness, honesty, modesty, gratitude, and reliability begin to evolve. Virtues are will that has been worked through with thought, will that is spirit-permeated.

Virtues are of great significance for an individual. Are a person's actions determined by outer conditions, waves of emotion, habits, or momentary irritation? If the impulses of justice, loyalty, or honesty are at work in his deeds, he acts completely out of himself. Human will receives inner form through virtue; our actions gain an inner certainty. The French psychologist Le Senne once characterized virtues as "the inner skeleton of the soul."

This inner skeleton is formed—as is the final configuration of the physical skeleton—through certain transformative processes.[5] Virtues are developed through the transformation of other soul traits. Modesty is developed by overcoming inordinate desire. Reliability is developed if a person no longer allows his actions to be determined by ever-changing experiences of sympathy and antipathy. And the virtue of diligence is attained when a person transforms indolence and sluggishness through the power of intention. When we understand the human soul, we see that every virtue corresponds to a weakness and that often an inner struggle takes place between the weakness and its corresponding virtue. Desire, sympathies and antipathies, indolence, the tendency to react emotionally, all are elementary driving forces of the astral body. They are transformed into human virtues through a slow metamorphosis, deep in the human soul. The individual acts out of the dynamic core of selfhood in this process of transformation, a process of overcoming. As the force of selfhood grows, the ego slowly permeates the astral body. Thus a person who acts with deliberation, carefulness, or uprightness acts completely out of himself. He has freed himself from the chains of stupefying urges.

Just as the ego permeates the body by transforming inherited forms, it now permeates the astral body. This brings about inner harmony between selfless thoughts and will, which, as virtue, forms an inner moral realm. The inner life of the individual takes on a moral character.[6]

Moral Education in the Second Seven Years

How can we support these processes through education? How can the development of moral character traits be nurtured in schools? This facet of education affects the individuality more strongly than other educational tasks and confronts educators with a challenge that must, for the most part, be met before the child reaches puberty. There are specific axioms of life that govern moral education. Rudolf Steiner characterized one of them as follows:

When we want to educate a child, whenever we believe that she should acquire this or that character attribute, we must approach the child indirectly, so to say. We should not try to graft this or that attribute upon the child, but we first should awaken the yearning for this trait; we should first get the child to yearn for acquiring this characteristic later on.

And a little later he added: "If we are able to guide a child's desires, we affect the core of a child's life."[7]

A desire or a longing can be awakened in a child's soul only through intense encounters. The strongest possible feeling for the significance of virtue must be awakened in children. Plutarch, for instance, was convinced of this. He begins his description of Pericles' life with the following comment:

Virtuous action affects us in such a way that we do not merely marvel at the deeds, but wish to imitate those who have done them.... For the good attracts us powerfully... it forms the character of those who observe it not only when they imitate it, the observation alone awakens a quality of resolve. This has moved me to continue my biographies of famous men.[8]

The predisposition for and the seeds of morality are present in a child's soul. When children experience morality in their encounters with the world around them, these seeds are awakened and brought to life. Initially this takes place in their encounters with adults, including their teachers. As Steiner wrote, "We should praise that human being and call him fortunate, who is able to look up to his teachers and educators as natural authorities—not only in the special moments of life, but always."[9]

In a time in which children are exposed through the media to images of untransformed forces of the soul, to licentious action and brutality, a teacher needs a strong inner preparation to be able to counter the effects of this mis-education. In striving toward a moral education, he may immerse himself intensely in the images of fairy tales and legends and in the figures of mythology and history. He first learns to experience deeply within himself what lives in them as virtue, transformed soul forces, and moral strength. Then his storytelling will be permeated with the experience of this majesty and strength. It is only thus that a teacher's words can find their way into the deeper soul regions of a child in which the seeds of morality lie. By living into the experience of the these images, children find themselves moved to look up to figures in the stories and discover an inner sympathy, an inclination for what lives in them as moral strength. The emotional nature of this inclination can cover the entire spectrum from gentle sympathy to a feeling of being thunderstruck. In these encounters of the soul, the seeds of morality sprout in each child differently and with a different intensity.

The soul opens itself through emotions to the manifold world of moral forces. In this emotional opening, longing to develop these forces awakens in our own souls.

Strengthening the Seed of Morality in Sleep

Longings, unlike momentary waves of feeling, do not dissipate quickly; they live on in the soul, giving its striving an inner direction, even when it is no longer stimulated from without. When addressing questions of moral education and the development of a moral disposition, we must take into account a recurring phase of daily life that poses a riddle to our normal consciousness: sleep.

When a human being falls asleep, his inner being releases itself from its connection to the physical body. This being can be recognized in the waking individual in many ways: in posture, expression, gesture, voice, action, and so on. In sleep, the body is like an empty container. The ego and the astral body are in some degree freed from it. For a time, they exist beyond the influences that affect them in waking; they exist within a lawfulness that is innate to them. Through this shift in the modality of existence, much is clarified that was still confused as we passed into sleep. Thoughts and judgments take on breadth and depth. Emotions, which may have held the soul captive, recede; their insignificance becomes apparent. At times, one arises from sleep with new goals and resolutions. Sleep provides a deeper awakening and a space for inner work.

Where does this take place? Who participates in these vital processes? The ego and the astral body enter an environment that is fundamentally different from the natural world. Spirit manifests itself in the natural world through the earthly media of matter and force. A human being cannot become conscious of the earthly world without his body. In the world that the human being enters in sleep, beings live who do not need a body to apply their gifts or to develop their capacities. These are beings with stronger inner forces. The concept of evolution can aid in understanding these beings.

In the future, according to Steiner, human beings will evolve to higher stages. The next stage is that of the spirit-self.[10] The beings higher than humans, the beings of the so-called third hierarchy, have already developed the spirit-self and, in part, still higher spiritual forces. Steiner wrote about the spirit-self in *Theosophy*: The fact that the spirit-self is developed "becomes apparent in so far as instincts, drives, and passions become translucent, illuminated by that which the 'I' has received from spirit." As with development of character virtues, we look to transformation of the astral body: Urges, desires, and passions are the forces of impulse that live in the astral body. They are dark and of glowing intensity. The darkness is illuminated by the spiritual light, which the "I" has taken up into itself and transformed in a process of transubstantiation.

In moments of passion, one gives oneself completely to an experience of enjoyment; the astral body flares up in the licentious enjoyment of sensual experience. This flaring up can be illuminated by the spiritual light of truth and moral ideals. The more comprehensive the truth and the higher the ideal, the more able they are to permeate the heat of passion. In this process the warmth of passion unites itself with the truth, with the moral ideal. The soul begins to glow with the warmth of its devotion to the spirit. The hot coals of passion become the selfless flame of enthusiasm.

A dull impetus, without form or direction, works in the realm of the urges. These too can be illuminated by the spiritual light with which the "I" fills itself. Unarticulated will then frees itself from the body. It unites its strength with the light of truth and of ideals. The undirected impetus becomes inner striving, striving to realize the spirit within our own will. Thus urges become transformed into a form of spiritual service.

Desire also becomes a significant capacity in the realm of the spirit-self. In contrast to urges, desire flares up in relation to surroundings. It draws those things toward itself that it seeks to turn into itself in search of satisfaction. The consuming energy of desire can be satisfied only momentarily. Transformed, however, desire becomes the kind of devotion through which one takes the spirit into oneself in such a way that one experiences bliss. Desire becomes the soul's inner force of devotion to the spirit.

These three traits—selfless enthusiasm, inner spiritual devotion, and striving to reveal the spirit-self in action—characterize the beings of the third hierarchy. Because they have transformed the astral body into the spirit-self, their being is living morality.

Children enter the realm of these beings when they sleep. They bring with them the qualities of sympathy and will-directed inclination for the morals that have been awakened in them through their lessons. This gives them a certain openness to the beings of the third hierarchy. In that children have been touched by virtues, that is, by the forces of morality, an inner relationship lives in children's astral bodies to these beings, beings who are no longer at the stage of striving for morality but rather have enabled morality to ripen within them. This allows the beings of the third hierarchy to bring their forces to bear on the seeds of morality, to enliven them, and to strengthen them. Significant processes of moral development unfold in the course of this nightly communication between the inner beings of children and higher beings.

What is enlivened and strengthened in sleep by the moral forces of higher beings flows into the waking life of a child. It is possible to recognize the slow maturing of a child's moral forces. A child's behavior changes slowly. Bad habits or character traits recede or disappear altogether, positive activity appears. For instance, a child begins to share the feelings of others more than before, another begins to enjoy being able to help. Another appears to be more focused and undertakes more seriously to do what she says she will. In such instances we see the budding of the seeds of moral forces in a child. We can also see, at times, that a child's inclination toward what is good or noble becomes a basic mood of soul.

These outer changes are connected to changes in life processes, in the etheric body. Feelings always modify the rhythm of breathing. What come to expression are qualities of serenity or stimulation inherent in various feeling states. Breathing rhythm becomes increasingly peaceful or excited, its amplitude increases or decreases. Feelings immerse themselves in the living rhythm of the breathing process. Their effects disappear with the same rapidity as do the feelings themselves. If, however, in sleep, the child's relationship to what is good and noble is deepened through the beings of the third hierarchy, a child's astral body immerses itself with strengthened sympathy in the child's breathing life. Soul forces can become so strong that they do not merely modify the rhythm momentarily, but rather immerse themselves fully in this life of rhythm. They then live on in the form of a fine modification of a child's breathing. Sympathy for the moral is now present in a medium whose rhythm continues unbroken. It no longer dies away, but lives on in the flowing rhythm of the stream of breathing; it becomes a basic mood of soul.

Human Conscience

As educators, we must also keep in mind that an inner source of moral impulses exists in each human being: the human conscience. When a person whose heart has not grown entirely cold notices another person in need, what speaks within him at that moment is the voice of his conscience. If we pass by without reaching out to help, conscience speaks again, with similar incisiveness. Conscience is a source of moral impulses and of moral judgment. It speaks with the certainty of inspiration. It points us with irresistible force in the direction of moral action. The German philosopher J.G. Fichte wrote of conscience: "To listen to my conscience, to obey it honestly, without fear or cleverness, this is my only goal, my *raison d'etre*. My life has thus ceased to be an empty game devoid of truth or meaning." [11]

Many philosophers and psychologists have explored the nature of this inner moral voice, often asking where it is located within the human constitution. Some hold to the view that it is to be found within the realm of feeling. The voice of conscience is perceived in the emotional sphere. Conscience does not, however, belong to the circle of other emotions. It is different from emotions such as joy, sorrow, hope, reverence, and love. We experience in these emotions our own being. Conscience speaks in human souls with an objectivity that supersedes the merely personal. Other thinkers have placed conscience in the will, not in the sphere of will as it is manifested in daily activity, but in a higher form of will, for conscience commands the will. It is the origin of the deepest moral impulses. It appears to be rooted in the depths of the will. From there, it rises to the surface of consciousness in the emotional realm, where we experience it as a source of direction for our personal life.

The development of human conscience presents a burning question today. The voice of conscience can fall silent. The consequent lack of moral orientation creates a vacuum that can give rise to destructive forces of behavior. How does conscience develop? What can education do to help its development? Take, for example, the situation in which the inner disposition for what is good comes to life in the soul of a child and moves the child to help or protect another child. The impulses of helping and protecting penetrate the child's will like rays of light. When this child falls asleep, she bears with her, in her astral body and in her ego, will that has been permeated by moral action. This enters the world of the third hierarchy. There the beings of the third hierarchy can work with the strength of their spiritually permeated morality on the goodness living in the child's being. Into the child's will flow the strength and certitude of the moral. The child bears the effects of this encounter into her world when she awakes. What has been impressed upon the child from out of the realm of sublime moral will expresses itself within her as the voice of conscience.[12] Fichte characterized this dimension of the human conscience as "an oracle from the eternal world that reveals to me how to take my place within the order of the spiritual world."[13]

In Steiner's view, cultivating and nurturing the forces of human conscience belong to the challenge of moral education. This significantly widens the spectrum of what we have described. If conscience is to be developed further, a child must gain not only an emotional disposition that inclines toward what is good, but this disposition must also find its way into the will in the form of moral impulses. A child receives the strongest stimulation toward moral action from adults whom he learns to acknowledge as moral authorities based on the selfless nature of their actions. A child carries moral will impulses, sparked by meeting such individuals, into her sleep life, where these impulses are permeated with the moral strength of the third hierarchy. Thus, much depends on the adults and teachers in a child's life. The formation of conscience lies in the hands of educators.

The moral certitude that a child develops through the development of her conscience is brought to her consciousness by a specific organ. This organ is a metamorphosis of the will organization; conscience develops through acts of will born of the warmth of moral ideals. Formative activity of the will manifests itself directly in the contractile properties of muscles. Muscles are permeated by moral force when a person acts without thought for himself. The organ of conscience is a muscular organ. It must, however, be free from all activity that reaches into the outer world. It must have a relationship to feeling, for conscience speaks to us in the realm of emotion. Feelings express themselves inwardly through rhythm. Thus, the organ in which impulses of will—which originate in the spiritual—are perceived as the voice of conscience is a rhythmically pulsating muscle: the heart. When a child awakens in the morning and carries enlivened forces of conscience into the world, she becomes conscious of these impulses in her heart. Just as the enduring inclination of the soul toward what is good lives on in a child's breathing, the voice of conscience speaks in the rhythm of a child's heart. Moral education brings about a significant development within the rhythmic organization, in the etheric body. "We must attain morality through an inner development of rhythm in the years between ages seven and fourteen."[14]

Dangers in Adolescence

The challenges of moral education described here lie between the ages of seven and fourteen. Until the second dentition, the formation of the physical body predominates. From then until puberty, development of etheric life processes and rhythms in the organs of the torso hold sway. In the early years of childhood, the physical body takes on a configuration that allows it to be the basis of moral action. In the middle years, we work through education to ensure that a strong connection to what is moral is created in rhythmic processes of the etheric. This is important for our path through life.

In the transition from childhood to youth, forces awaken within human beings that endanger the possibility of a sound ethical existence. What has to be achieved by this point Steiner characterized in this way:

> ...The focus of education must be such that when an individual passes through puberty he has a strong feeling: I am not a whole human being, I don't have the right to call myself a human being, if I am not good.

Young persons need a strongly conscious, deeply felt awareness that being human and acting morally are inseparable. This orients them so that they do not to fall prey to dangers threatening their moral capabilities.

During puberty, elemental forces of the astral body burst into the soul life of the youth—sensuality, passions, desires. Other soul qualities also arise: ideals, the capacity for enthusiasm, an inner search for meaning. These latter are forces of the astral body that have already been transformed and spiritualized. Thus, young adults experience a strong inner tension and disharmony. If they find nothing within to serve as their inner compass, they can easily find themselves in danger.

In order to describe these dangers adequately, we must summon a seemingly antiquated concept that has virtually disappeared from our vocabulary. It is common today to use the word "evil" to describe the horrible events of the last century; the term "sin," however, is seldom used. Ambrosius, one of the Catholic patriarchs in the fourth century, listed the seven mortal sins as lust, gluttony, greed, sloth, wrath, envy, and pride. In lust, a person loses himself in the desires and passions of sexuality. Gluttony is unbridled enjoyment of the desires of eating and drinking. In greed, a person is trapped by the urge to possess. Sloth is passive surrender to bodily pleasure. When a person surrenders himself to the untransformed forces of his astral body, to those drives which he shares with the animals, he falls into sin. He forgets the actual task of being human: the gradual transformation of these forces into moral capacities.

In a comprehensive study of changes in adolescent behavior we find the following:

> ... [A] monopoly that is toppled: access to the pleasures and privileges of adults. To be an adult once meant having access to sexual relationships....With the end of patronized youth, the lusts and pleasures are moved more closely into the vicinity of childhood.

> Sexuality and erotic relationships are only one example. Even adult forms of oral gratification have become available to younger children. Ever more young people are smoking and drinking, visiting bars and night-clubs, and finding access to the drug culture and addictions....[15]

One of the most worrisome tendencies of modern culture is described here in the dry style of contemporary sociological studies: the propagation of temptation and the opportunity to surrender oneself without orientation to that world of temptation. The path into what we should actually term the realm of sin is being trodden, unheeded, as though it were the most natural way in the world. MacIntyre characterized this trend quite accurately when he remarked that today thinking and speaking about morality have been "abandoned."[16]

Commandments cannot help in the battle against temptation. Human beings no longer allow themselves be directed from without. They need a direction, an orientation that comes from within.

The second danger comes from the realm of destructive instincts. What we speak of as evil can work demonically, to the degree it has in the last century, only when it arises within human beings. Individuals find themselves confronted by forces from which they previously felt protected. These, too, emerge in the transition from childhood to youth. Many examples point clearly to this, especially the tendency toward brutality apparent at this age. We may also include the peculiar interest in horror films, with their terrifying images of torture, injury, and destruction. No young persons would have an inclination to watch such images if there were not within them, somewhere, a lust for evil. This demonic lust is drawn out by films. Psychologists speak of an enjoyment of fear, because the experience of fear is connected to this feeling of enjoyment. None would experience such a feeling of lust for evil, did they not bear within themselves an inner power of destruction. Individuals need this power, but it should not become a basis for action. In one of the most important works of Jewish mysticism, the Sohar, stands the statement:

> Evil is necessary, because God wanted to give humans freedom of choice. For this reason alone he had to want the existence of evil, in order that in resisting evil man could save and strengthen his moral forces.[17]

Humans beings bear evil within themselves not in order to act destructively, but, by resisting it, to develop forces of good in inner independence and freedom. The instincts and drives of evil work in the depths of human souls. It is a tragedy, however, when they rise up in the soul and the lust for evil or destructive instincts become the basis for action. Adolescents are not mature enough to face them alone. In watching horror films, for example, they may come to the point articulated by one adolescent: "Everything in me is erased by these films."[18] What are erased are human emotions of compassion and the ability to have sympathy for others. A moral vacuum appears within the individual.

Where does evil originate within a human being? In the processes of change which take place during puberty, youth comes into an unmediated relationship with the forces of gravity. Adolescent growth spurts begin with the bones of the limbs, that is, with those parts of the body which, due to their tendency toward crystallization, separate themselves most strongly from the inner life of the individual. Because of their density, limb bones are more strongly affected by gravity. Gravity concentrates matter toward the center of the earth. It leads through concentration to solidification and separation from the rest of the cosmos. As bones grow, this force exercises a greater influence on the individual, and the will becomes focused, through the muscles, ever more strongly on overcoming weight and inertia. Adolescents unite their wills with those forces that would draw them out of a connection with the cosmos. As they permeate their will with forces of gravity, they gain a stronger feeling for themselves. In unconscious depths of the will, a form of egotism emerges which is drawn only to itself. If this finds its way into consciousness, it becomes an urge to destroy everything that is not in harmony with our own egotism. A destructive hate rises from unconscious depths. This power of destruction should remain in depths of soul, coming to consciousness only as an enhanced sense of self that supports the development of an independent personality.

Today, as these forces find their way to the surface and endanger humanity, education finds itself facing new challenges. Two things are important in striving toward a form of education that can help adolescents stand up to the threats of this inner source of evil: Adolescents must learn to understand the world so deeply that they find an inner connection to it, and they must learn to grow beyond themselves in order to place themselves in the larger context of life and the cosmos.[19]

Endnotes

1. Novalis, *Werke*. Herausgegeben und kommentien von G. Schulz. München o. J., S. 560.
   Novalis, Works, edit and commentary by G. Schulz, Munich, no year, p. 560.
2. In German, *"das Ich"* translates literally as "the I," but we have substituted the more common "ego," "self," or "selfhood," depending on use, for common understanding. The use of ego in this case, however, does not connote what psychoanalysts mean by the term.
3. E.-M. Kranich, "Entwicklung und Erziehung in der frühen Kindheit" in: S. Leber (Hrsg.), *Die Pädagogik der Waldorfschule und Ihre Grundlagen,* 3. Aufl., Darmstadt, 1992.
   E.-M. Kranich, "Early Childhood Development and Education" in: S. Leber (ed.), *Waldorf Education and Its Foundations*, 3rd edition, Darmstadt, 1992.

4. Ders., "Die Kräfte leiblicher Form-bildung und ihre Umwandlung in die Fähigkeit, Formen zu gestalten und zu erleben," in: E.-M. Kranich u.a., *Formenzeichnen*, 2. Aufl., Stuttgart, 1992. O.D. Creutzfeld, *Cortex Cerebri*. Berlin, Heidelberg, New York, 1983, S. 311.
   Same Author, "The Forces of Bodily Form-giving and Their Transmutation into the Ability to Shape and Experience Form" in: E.-M. Kranich et al. *Form Drawing*, 2nd edition. Stuttgart, 1992. O.D. Creutzfeld, *Cortex Cerebri*. Berlin, Heidelberg, New York, 1983, p. 311.
5. Siehe A.R. Luria, *Die höheren kortikalen Funktionen des Menschen und ihre Störungen bei örtlichen Hirnschädigungen*. Berlin, 1970. O. D. Creutzfeldt, Berlin, Heidelberg, New York, 1983, J.M. Foster, *The Prefrontal Cortex*. New York, 1989.
   See A.R. Luria, *The Higher Cortical Functions of the Human Being and Their Disturbance in the Case in Localized Brain Damage*. Berlin 1970. O.D. Creutzfeld, *Cortex Cerebri*, Berlin, Heidelberg, New York, 1983. J.M. Foster, *The Prefrontal Cortex*, New York, 1989.
6. A precise description of the field termed "astral body" can be found in Rudolf Steiner's *Theosophy*. GA 9, Dornach, 1987, p. 56 ff.
7. Rudolf Steiner, *Der Christus-Impuls und die Entwicklung des Ich-Bewusstseins* (*The Christ-Impulse and the Development of the "I" Consciousness*). GA 116, Dornach, 1982, p. 48f.
8. Plutarch, *Lebensbeschreibungen*, Bd.1. München, 1964, S. 317.
   Plutarch, *The Lives of Great Men,* vol. 1. Munich, 1964, p. 317.
9. Rudolf Steiner, "Die Erziehung des Kindes vom Gesichtspunkte der Geisteswissenschaft" in: *Luzifer-Gnosis*. GA 34, Dornach,1987, S.330.
   Rudolf Steiner "The Education of the Child from the Viewpoint of Spiritual Science" in *Lucifer-Gnosis*. GA 34, Dornach, 1987, p. 330.
10. They are termed Life-Spirit (*Lebensgeist*) and Spirit-Man (*Geistesmensch*). See commentary of Rudolf Steiner in *Theosophy*. Note 5, pp. 53ff and 59.
11. J. G. Fichte, *Die Bestimmung des Menschen* (*The Destiny of Man*), 5th edition. Hamburg, 1979, p. 94 f.
12. See Rudolf Steiner's comment in *Anthroposophie als Kosmosophie* (*Anthroposophy as Cosmosophy*), Zweiter Teil (part two). Lecture of November 12, 1921, in Dornach. GA 208, Dornach 1992.
13. Quoted from H. Reiner, "Gewissen" ("Conscience") in *Historisches Wörterbuch der Philosophie*. Bd. 3. Darmstadt 1974, S. 586. H. Reiner, "Conscience" in *Historical Dictionary of Philosophy*, vol. 3. Darmstadt, 1974, p. 586.
14. Rudolf Steiner, *Geistige Zusammenhänge in der Gestaltung des menschlichen Organismus. (Spiritual Interconnections in the Formation of the Human Organism)*. Lecture of December 9, 1922, in Stuttgart. GA 218, Dornach, 1992, p. 325.
15. Ibid., p. 328f.

16. *Jugend '81*. Jugendwerk der Deutschen Shell, Opladen, 1982, S. 99. (*Youth '81*. Youth Foundation of German Shell Co., Opladen, 1982, p. 99.)
17. Quoted from G. Sholem, *Die jüdische Mystik in ihren Hauptströmungen* (*Major Trends in Jewish Mysticism*), German edition. Frankfurt a.M., 1967, p. 261.
18. See also here J. Loesch, "Horror und Gewaltfilme in einer Haupt und Realschule" ("Horror Movies and Violent Films in a German School") in *Pädagogik* 11/1992, p.12 ff.
19. This aspect of moral education is the topic of my article, "Der Weg zum Verstehen der Natur als Prozeß moralischer Entwicklung" ("The Path to Understanding Nature as a Process of Moral Development").

Conscience and Morality

by

Karl Brodersen

translated by Ted Warren

What is conscience? What is morality? We need go no further than an unanswered letter, a postponed visit to an elderly relative, or a regretful word. In truth every minute of our lives is full of undone deeds. We always have good excuses: I had too much to do, my back hurt, I was in shock, I was bothered by my concerns for others, or in our childhood we were spoiled, abandoned or abused. This all affects our moral life. Does this affect our conscience, does our conscience even care what other people do or do not do? Maybe not, but we are very concerned with it. We are hiding something from our spouses, cheating on our taxes if we have the chance. We lie here, act mean there, put a little water in the wine, and it is all so human. We continuously forgive ourselves and put our conscience at ease.

Does everyone have a conscience? There are huge differences between people. Interestingly, the nicest, gentlest among us have the most tender conscience. They experience guilt when no one else would even think about it. Are guilty feelings primarily created in childhood? With the word *conscience* we usually mean a guilty conscience, but does it not also have a totally different side? Does it not stimulate us to do good deeds, to love others? As children we are not only disciplined but we are loved, we are cared for by loving mothers and by others. We can argue whether mother love is an instinct or a moral power. Instead let us hear what great spirits have thought and spoken on the subject.

Two Danish theologians, Lars Bo Bojesen and Jan Lindhardt, wrote an excellent book on how great thinkers have understood conscience.[1] It appeared in Copenhagen in 1979 under the title *Conscience*. They begin with the time from just before year 1 AD until the middle of the nineteenth century, during which time pagans and Christians alike considered conscience to be an almighty, admonishing sun that shone upon all mankind, enlightening hearts as to what is right and what is wrong. Conscience was God's voice in our hearts reflected in individual human souls. Passing over the Ancient Greek thinkers, they quote the stoic Seneca, at the time of Jesus. In the forty-first letter to his old friend Lucilius, he wrote:

> We do not need to raise our hands to heaven, nor ask the temple servant for a place to lie before the picture of God in order to be more readily heard. God is near you, He is with you, and He is inside of

you. Lucilius, I think that within us sits the Holy Spirit, who observes our bad and good deeds and watches over us; as it is treated by us so does it treat us in return. I am certain that no one can be a good man without the help of God. Do you believe anyone can rise above fate without His help? In every good man a good God lives, but what type of God we do not know.

In Romans, Chapter 2, St Paul discussed the difference between Jews and Gentiles:

For when the Gentiles, which have not the law, do by nature the things contained in the law, these, having not the law, are a law unto themselves. Which shows the work of the law written in their hearts, their *conscience* also bearing witness, and their thoughts the means for accusing or else excusing one another.

St Paul used the Greek word *synderesis* [the principle in moral consciousness which directs an agent to good] twelve times in his letters, but he does not attach any perfection to conscience. Rather he speaks a number of places about conscience's uncertainty. The Church Father Origines (who died in 254) spoke of St Paul: "I think that *conscience* is the spirit in the soul that discovers, accompanies and guides us. Its task is to provide us with the best course of action and to correct us when we have sinned."

Two hundred years later Hieronymus of Rhodes, an Aristotelian philosopher, wrote a comment on the prophets:

These authors interpret visions in agreement with Plato's theory on the three elements of the soul: reason, spirit [will] and desire. These represent respectfully the human being, the lion and the bull. Above them is the eagle. Just as there is an element above all three elements, there is also a fourth element that the Greeks called *synderesis*. It is the spark of conscience that was never put out, not even in Cain's heart as he was driven out of the fields. It is makes us feel our sinfulness when we are overcome by evil desires or unrestricted spirit or are fooled by seductive reason. It is natural to identify *synderesis* with the eagle since it is different than all other elements and connects them when they make mistakes.

The Scholastic's treatment of this question is presented and material on the realism of St Thomas Aquinas (*via antiqua*) and William of Occam's nominalistic picture of conscience (*via moderna*). On St Thomas:

In the end you would ask how Christian theology influenced his concept of conscience that we have so far described as a purely human endeavor. Roughly stated it can be said that revelations do not follow something new to natural law, and therefore do not increase ethical knowledge. Everything written so far is true to the same degree for Gentiles as for Christians. But something new appears with Christ. The Christian receives the Holy Spirit, whose mercy is embodied in us (*art habitus*) and makes us want to act correctly. It makes us feel free to act in a way that pleases mercy and avoids that which acts against mercy.

The will becomes supported and guided by this new entity that is identical with God's love. People no longer observe their conscience's messages as a necessity they must follow, but as something they freely act upon, happily and willingly. Now it is more evident than ever before that conscience is free and sovereign. Under the ancient law to which Jewish people were bound, people were subjected to many outer restrictions and commandments. All that is gone now, and only conscience remains, with love as its companion and helpmate to realize its free insights.

Occam is sumarized as follows: "It appears to me that Occam prematurely grasps the way future thinkers defined conscience as the unbeatable power in the human mind and yet learned and determined by experiences. Shall we not look to Freud to find the parallel?" The section on Scholasticism is concluded: "According to both *via antiqua* and *via moderna*, Hieronymus' eagle has landed and created a home in the human being."

A major force of change at the end of the Middle Ages, Occam died in 1348. Then the whole question of the being of conscience and its role was reviewed on new premises. People began to view themselves and the world with a new form of self-conscience. Martin Luther appeared as the herald of this new age. When asked to retract his thesis during a session of parliament in Worms in 1521, he spoke: "Retract them I cannot nor do I want to, as it is dangerous and inadvisable to act against one's conscience."

But one thing is an attitude that is expressed with words and another is Luther's theology and its interpretation of the role conscience plays. Here he does not speak of conscience as a God-inspired ability to discern between right and wrong as did St Thomas, but rather as an eternal reminder of our status as fallen, guilty and sinful beings. We find that interpretation of Lutheran thought in all Protestant theology; something that easily transitions into a religion of laws that searches for support in the moral life, not as St Thomas did in the heart of man enlightened by the Holy Ghost, but rather in the scriptures and the church's authority, much like Occam's divine command interpretation. In reality the distinction and division between both opinions is not as sharp as indicated. Life provides its own corrections regardless of the theology. Eventually life becomes the center of our attention. All speculative and dogmatic thinking recedes, making room for objective thinking as natural science fills our spiritual horizon. The human being and his soul life become the objects of the same kind of thinking that takes on gravity, magnetism and microbes.

In this new way of thinking, we find a new way to think of conscience. An important example is given from Jean-Jacques Rousseau's statements on the rights of individuals and children from *Emile, or On Education*, first published in 1762. In the fourth book we find Rousseau's confrontation with theology in the form of a Savoyard priest's lecture on knowledge and conscience. Here we find the following praise of conscience:

> Conscience! Conscience! Godly instinct, eternal and heavenly voice, you secure the path for an ignorant and limited but thoughtful and free being, perfect judge of good and evil that makes mankind godlike, it is you who places the godliness in his nature and morality in his deeds; without you I would feel nothing within me that raises me above animals—nothing more than the advantage of flapping around from craziness to craziness, equipped as I am with a rational mind with no direction and rationality without principles.

With this belief in human perfection, St Thomas' *via antiqua* reappears, but now without the appearance of mercy. Conscience has become an attribute among people, their own property.

In multiple variations we find this opinion again amongst idealistic thinkers and the Romantic poets in the eighteenth and nineteenth centuries. From a colder perspective of the human soul and its deeds in history, new voices appear. Bojesen has collected them in the chapter "Conscience as a Product" and includes the most famous voices of this conviction: Karl Marx, Friedrich Nietzsche and Sigmund Freud. Citing Arthur Schopenhauer, Bojesen describes the leading opinions regarding conscience: "Many people will wonder if they realized that their conscience, so stately it appears to him, actually is a combination of approximately one-fifth human fear, one-fifth superstition, one-fifth prejudice, one-fifth conceit, and one-fifth habit, so that he is no better than the Englishman who said: I cannot afford to keep a conscience."

Marx did not pay much attention to conscience in his writings, but one quote says a lot: "A republican has a different conscience than a royalist, an owner has a different conscience than one who owns nothing, a thinking person a different one than someone who does not think." But Marx considered conscience to be a significant political factor. "If an entire nation was seriously ashamed of itself, it would be like a lion that contracts its body before it pounces."

Through education and propaganda one creates a political experience of shame. The background for this is old methods used by the Christian Evangelists. In his later works Nietzsche goes so far as to declare morality as a source of power that uses the conscience to hold weak people in an iron grip. The strong ones, however, free themselves from this dishonesty and on behalf of their will for power, declare themselves free of guilt: "Atheism and a certain reborn innocence belong together."

Bojesen dives into Freud's interpretation of conscience: guilt and morality, summarizing:

Freud asked himself the same question as Nietzsche: How can conscience be strongest among the most cultivated and morally educated people? He then answered in the direction of some of Nietzsche's thoughts. The beginning of conscience, according to Nietzsche, is the violent repression of human instincts that occurs suddenly when they should be positioned to peaceful and regulated social norms. Instincts are repressed in their outward expression but turned inward where they rage with conscience rigidity against the human being, torturing him with powerful feelings of guilt. As they say Nietzsche thinks extremely psychologically. The only difference is in the technical terminology when Freud determines that the strict conscience is a result of repressed aggression within the Super-Ego.

And finally: "Conscience appeared in that context as something extremely relevant, and the removal of its demand for absolute trust that had been previously prepared guided Freud through his argument that human conscience is a product of the psychological milieu it finds itself living within."

Bojesen and Lindhardt end their history with a chapter devoted mostly to Søren Kierkegaard, which opens with the following citation from his diary in 1849:

> People say that everyone has conscience and consider it a prerequisite, yet there is no *attribute* (neither a physical such as dancing or singing, nor a spiritual such as thinking and similar activities) that demands such a *long* and *difficult schooling* before a human can say he *has conscience*. Just as pure gold is mixed with all kinds of impure and uncommon materials, so it is with conscience in its immediate condition, where it consists of elements that are the opposite of conscience. Therein lies what Hegel considers conscience as a form of evil. On the other hand, this is irresponsibly labeled. He should have rather said: What many call conscience is absolutely not conscience, but warm vapors from the stomach—bailiff's conscience.
>
> We must admit that eternity, in which each person will be judged, will demand that every human being has created a conscience. That will be the main judgment: have you had a conscience or not: but take note that if you did not, definitely you are judged.

With such words Kierkegaard neutralized the scientific reductionism that held sway in the second half of the nineteenth century and dominated our spiritual horizon. Kierkegaard approved all those who in the name of genetic biology, sociology and psychology define the human being as a more or less well-outfitted animal and consider conscience to be an inbuilt reflection of that outfit. This is what he points to with his "bailiff's conscience." But what did Kierkegaard think are the distinctions of true conscience and how do we obtain it? To answer that question one needs to work with his entire lifework, which builds upon his key concept of *choice*. What Kierkegaard placed in that word is very hard to capture, but let us make an attempt, as presented by Lindhardt:

> Kierkegaard solves this problem rather simply. Only that which the individual himself has chosen can be called his own. Therefore you must choose in order to have a conscience. You must choose to be talented, to be in love, to have parents, etc. But one may protest that we have received all of these things—we cannot do anything for being equipped in one way or another, nor for finding ourselves in one situation or the other. No, that is it, answers Kierkegaard. It is absolutely correct that you are something previously, something very specific, but all that you can only make your own if you choose to do so. It is not the prerequisites but the adoption of such that makes a human being ruler over things and thus his own ruler. As a product he is stuck between the forms of reality. In the choice he makes himself elastic, transforms his entire outer world to his inner world.

The voice of conscience is therefore merely vapor or "arisen from the stomach" until the person *decides* that he will have a conscience and that he will obey his voice. Kierkegaard became even more radical than Rousseau. For him it was the human being that not only has a conscience but—correctly understood—also brings it forth:

> The choice immediately makes two dialectical movements, one that chooses or else it was not a choice. If that which I chose was not there, then I did not choose, I created but I did not create myself, I chose myself. Just as nature is created out of nothingness (by God's creation), just as I, as an immediate personality, am created out of nothingness, so am I as a free spirit born of contradictory elements, or born because I chose myself.
>
> Of what I have written it sounds as if we choose to have a conscience, in other words there is no element of content in conscience. Now Kierkegaard's pattern of thought is much more complicated and varied than I can express properly. But I believe that it is correct to propose that one of his points is that there is not such a great difference between knowing and choosing. In the second part of his essay "Either This or That," he lets his ethical spokesman, accountant William, repeat the challenge from the Temple of Delphi: *Know Thyself*. The ethical individual knows himself, but the knowledge is merely contemplation (speculative observations). Thus the individual is determined according to its necessity, it is a recollection of himself, where the Self is an action, and therefore I have used the expression to choose yourself, rather than knowing yourself.

It is not easy to get hold of what lies in these words in Kierkegaard's typical formulations. A gifted man in Norway said that thinking is born when you fall down the steps, so in order to pick up the thread we should return to the starting point of our observations that were our own, immediate, and daily experiences. Let us begin by compare the Danish formulation: "It is not the prerequisites but the adoption of such that makes a human being ruler over things and thus his own ruler," to Goethe's German formulation: "What you have from your fathers, obtain it, in order to own it."

And from our "fathers," our forefathers, we have received via inheritance and the environment most of what is our Self. But are we merely a product of the past, do we not add something new to our lives? No matter what our theories may be, we do believe we are responsible for our actions. If we follow a child's upbringing, we see how he or she takes responsibility for his or her life. A good education enables him to take over this responsibility, an education to freedom. Of course children must relate to their past. We cannot be our own creators, as Kierkegaard says, even though we must be creative with what we do inherit. From the child's first moment on earth, we observe it tirelessly working on the body and soul it has received. That activity is controlled. But by whom? Many believe it is controlled from the past, that a more or less effective program programs the child. But who programs our children? We shall let that question go unanswered for now in hope of adding more insight with further observations.

> Nineteenth century idealism reached its height on German ground with [Georg Wilhelm Friedrich] Hegel's theory that the *subjective* freedom was the highest possible expression of thought for freedom in our world, and therefore must be the absolute basis for a governmental and religious life. According to Hegel, it belongs to the "state of the modern world" that human beings are conscious, "that conscience is no longer related to a specific goal."
>
> The previously more sensory ages have something on the surface, something given before it, it may be religion or law but conscience in itself, as a thought, *and my thought alone is my duty.* In other words the human being has become his own lawgiver and brings from himself the highest ethical norm.

Bojesen's conclusion is somewhat misleading unless the reader is aware that for Hegel thinking is everything other than the fruit of subjective coincidences, but just the opposite, the human being's relationship to the highest God-like entity. With his thinking the individual represents his laws on earth. What that entailed for Hegel we cannot go into now, but take the citation as the expression for a life attitude that reached many people in the nineteenth century. How elementary that appears is illustrated in what Ellen Key expressed in her essays of 1898 in her account of a decisive experience from her youth:

> If I experienced thousands of years on the earth, I would never forget the time in my youth when the thought hit me that life could be art.

The revelation did not occur during a mystical experience but just as I left a choir practice! But it appeared with the entire dimension of a vision: to create a personality according to your ideals—that stand sculptured like an artist's prototype—and everything within the artistic area is aesthetic: I am the theme, the art is me, the broad public for which I create is me.

Other declarations by leading thinkers of the nineteenth century testify to how widely spread that attitude was. Kierkegaard is a good example and within the German cultural life we find Max Stirner and Nietzsche who demonstrate extreme individualism. In this milieu Rudolf Steiner appeared in 1894 with his *Philosophy of Freedom*, wherein he tried to explain and deepen philosophically what lived among the leading thinkers and spread as a wave of emancipation with no comparison in the history of mankind. Before we observe his writings on conscience, we can listen to his description of his book in the context of his times and his own life. In a letter to the author Rosa Mayreder (November 1894), he wrote: "I know exactly where my book belongs within the present streams of culture. I can put my finger on where it unites with Nietzsche's direction of thought. I can also say that I have expressed thoughts that are missing for Nietzsche. I can admit to my friends, but only to them—that it is painful for me that Nietzsche could not read my book. He could have taken it as it is: in every line a *personal* experience."

What is there to read on conscience in Steiner's book? Not much—the word is used only three times, first in the chapter called "The Idea of Freedom":

> There is a special kind of moral principle when the commandment is made known to us not through an external authority but through our own inner life (moral autonomy). In this case we hear the voice to which we have to submit ourselves, in our own souls. This voice expresses itself as *conscience*.
>
> It is a moral advance when a man no longer simply accepts the commands of an outer or inner authority as the motive of his action, but tries to understand the reason why a particular maxim of behavior should act as a motive in him. This is the advance from morality based on authority to action out of moral insight. [2]

Here we find in Steiner the same reservation that caused Kierkegaard to speak of a "bailiff's conscience." This contrasts what one would obtain by choosing, which would according to Kierkegaard demand knowledge or insight. By way of one's own insight an individual can change the given norms and messages to an individually proven attitude. There is much agreement between Kierkegaard's and Steiner's views of conscience and to the higher need for obtaining a conscience in modern times. Their language differs, but in common they share *insight* not as an empirical or rationally proven facility. Kierkegaard defined this as *choice* and Steiner as *moral intuition*.

Steiner included the idealistic philosopher Immanuel Kant in his cultural dialogues. His book is in answer to Kant's leading works, *The Criticism of Pure Reason* (1781) and *Criticism of Practical Reason* (1788). Steiner described the role of thinking in our understanding of the world and our selves. He then showed how thinking can become an organ for a moral insight through intuition. Because our thinking is mostly habitual and passively dependent on the use of fixed concepts within the language, we are not always clear about what role intuition plays in a true understanding, a personal acquirement of a concept. The basis for thinking can suddenly appear or it can be the fruits of observing one's own thinking in action.

In this respect *Philosophy of Freedom* was written to not only inform us of the problem but to give the reader an experience of the role of thinking which he needs to unite the right content with *intuition*. To demonstrate:

> In contrast to the content of the percept which is given to us from without, the content of thinking appears inwardly. The form in which this first makes its appearance we will call intuition. Intuition is for thinking what observation is for the percept. Intuition and observation are the sources of our knowledge. An observed object of the world remains unintelligible to us until we have within ourselves the corresponding intuition which adds that part of reality which is lacking in the percept. To anyone who is incapable of finding intuitions corresponding to the things, the full reality remains inaccessible.[3]
>
> What appears to us in observation as separate parts becomes combined, bit by bit, through the coherent, unified world of our intuitions. By thinking we fit together again into one piece all that we have taken apart through perceiving.[4]

Intuition receives the following meaning in our moral lives:

> Men vary greatly in their capacity for intuition. In one, ideas just bubble up; another acquires them with much labor. The situations in which men live and which provide the scenes of their actions are no less varied. The conduct of a man will therefore depend on the manner in which his faculty of intuition works in a given situation. The sum of ideas which are effective in us, the concrete content of our intuitions, constitutes what is individual in each of us, notwithstanding the universality of the world of ideas. Insofar as this intuitive content applies to action, it constitutes the moral content of the individual. To let this content express itself in life is both the highest moral driving force and the highest motive a man can have, who sees that in this content all other moral principles are in the end united. We may call this point of view *ethical individualism*.[5]

If a man acts only because he accepts certain moral standards, his action is the outcome of the principles which compose his moral code. He merely carries out orders. He is a superior automaton. Inject some stimulus to action into his mind, and at once the clockwork of his moral principles will set itself in motion and run its prescribed course, so as to result in an action which is Christian, or humane, or seemingly unselfish, or calculated to promote the progress of civilization. Only when I follow my love for my objective is it I myself who acts. I act, at this level of morality, not because I acknowledge a lord over me, or an external authority, or a so-called inner voice; I acknowledge no external principle for my action, because I have found in myself the ground for my action, namely, my love of the action.

I do not work out mentally whether my action is good or bad; I carry it out because I *love* it. My action will be "good" if my intuition, steeped in love, finds its right place within the intuitively experienceable world continuum; it will be "bad" if this is not the case. Again, I do not ask myself, "How would another man act in my position?"—but I act as I, this particular individuality, find I have occasion to do. No general usage, no common custom, no maxim applying to all men, no moral standard is my immediate guide but my love for the deed. I feel no compulsion, neither the compulsion of nature which guides me by my instincts, nor the compulsion of the moral commandments, but I want simply to carry out what lies within me. [6]

Under the impressions of Steiner's world of thought, some readers may be reminded of the following citation from St Thomas Aquinas that deserves to be repeated:

The Christian receives the Holy Spirit, whose mercy is embodied in us (*art habitus*) and makes us want to act correctly. It makes us feel free to act in a way that pleases mercy and avoids that which acts against mercy.

The will becomes supported and guided by this new entity that is identical with God's love. People no longer observe their conscience's messages as a necessity they must follow, but as something they freely act upon, happily and willingly. Now it is more evident than ever before that conscience is free and sovereign. Under the ancient law to which Jewish people were bound, people were subjected to many outer restrictions and commandments. All that is gone now, and only conscience remains, with love as its companion and helpmate to realize its free insights.

This is a motif that in demystified form has moved not only many thinkers but also the masses. For Rudolf Steiner it was the main motif for his life.

Did this quick passage though the history of the concept of conscience help us understand our own situation a little better, maybe not so much our private situation but rather one that all humanity now faces? Life has changed dramatically both within the material and social realms in such a way that wisdom from the past is problematical, if not useless. We cannot consider a future on earth if a moral source does not open our souls to what Steiner calls *moral imagination* in order to deal with the challenges. And this can happen only if individuals discover and assume their responsibility for the earth and mankind's well being. Or, to express it as Kierkegaard did, "obtain a conscience."

Endnotes
1. All material quoted, unless otherwise noted, is from *Samvittigheden* [*Conscience*] by Lars Bo Bojesen and Jan Lindhardt, Copenhagen: Berlingske Leksikon Bibliotek, 1979.
2. Steiner, Rudolf. *The Philosophy of Freedom*, translated by Michael Wilson, London: Rudolf Steiner Press, 1970, p. 131.
3. Ibid., p. 73.
4. Ibid., p. 74.
5. Ibid., p. 134.
6. Ibid., p. 136.

The West and East in Us

by

Jørgen Smit

translated by Ted Warren

Our modern civilization is the civilization of the West. It was created in Western Europe and North America. With irrepressible power, it has spread to the rest of the world. The extent to which Africa and Asia's folk enter the political and economic arena is determined by the extent to which they use the results and methods created by Western civilization. In the timeline of human development, there has been no alternative that has moved beside or past Western civilization. It is the most complicated civilization ever, and the complexity increases year to year.

These are the times of educated specialists in all areas and of the huge unspecialized, uneducated masses. All of our resources are directed toward one goal—to control outer reality and to reach to a position of comfort and security, maximum prestige and well-being. But how much is enough? How good is good enough? If we do not continually increase production every year, secure new heights in the world market, create ever-better products and improvements, we would quickly notice signs of a coming recession. The consistent, forward-moving will to control the outer world is the driving force behind the West.

Western civilization's domination over the East has been unstoppable. Just what happened in the twentieth century meeting of the West and East? Was the West's one-sided victory at the expense of an ancient culture that no longer had a future? Can the East's deepest, most authentic quality be united with the progressive line of the West? Will the East's valuable facets and worldview be shut down and replaced by the West's single-minded, world-dominating civilization?

The encounters between these two ways of life were especially confrontational and brutal at the end of the nineteenth century. For example, when the first telegraph line, a gift from the West, was set up between Fu-Tschou and Amoy, signs were posted all over Tschuan-Tschin:

> People of the villages, you are hereby called upon to resist the building of the "lightning threads." Everyone should know that barbarians have come here from an island beyond the four oceans to hurt us and ruin us by removing the peace and order that has sustained us for many generations.
>
> The line begins at the eastern gate of the capital of the province Fu-Tschou and is now set up in Hok Tschin. Where it is raised we find not a single piece of ground the size of an egg that is not damaged

forever. It throws shadows over our fathers' graves, damages our ownership rights, destroys *Feng-tschui* and brings sickness and death to our wives and children.

Our entire folk are enraged. Let the drums sound, strike the gongs, and let us awaken the whole nation to resistance. If anyone works with the barbarians, sells them land or rice or works for them, they shall be arrested immediately and mercilessly killed. Let us unite to resist the arrival of the barbarians. If they appear, attack them and murder them. This is a very important because our property and our lives are at stake and we should not be afraid of resisting and holding together.

Much the same could be read in the newspaper *Sin-pao*, when the drainage project in the Vusung River at the port of Shanghai was announced:

Mountains can be changed to valleys and deep valleys to mountains. The blue ocean can become fertile fields and fertile fields can become blue oceans. We know that the most beautiful harbors under the Ming-dynasty in the province of Kiangsu were along the Liu River. Huge ships swarmed in and merchants arrived in the thousands. The ships that transported the corn to the sea to Tientsin were loaded in the very same Liu River. At that time no one knew of Vusung. When the Liu River filled up with sand, they used the Vusung River. Thirty years ago the ships collected at Vusung (a village with the same name as the river), and the early life in the villages along the Liu River was removed from our memory. Thirty years is a man's age and here we may have seen the will of Heaven. According to Western concepts human accomplishment and willpower can overcome Heaven. But China is ruled in line with the commands from Heaven. Devoted obedience to Heaven determines everything we do. As Heaven decides, so it must be. If Heaven wants the Vusung River to fill with sand for thirty more years then it is unnecessary to dredge it. Heaven is not so weak that human beings can fight it.

This was all naturally a hopeless battle. Western civilization entered and China forced "the great leap forward." Now China's leaders consider atomic bombs important and do not ask whether or not they disturb nature's holy breath, *Feng-tschui*.

The spirit of the East will not disappear, even though it is gradually removed from the economic-social-political fields. Removal does not mean domination or destruction. It is suppression and sidetracking into the underconscious.

From the most surprising sources the spiritual life of the East appears in masked figures. Let us take one example: C.G. Jung, the Swiss doctor (1875–1961). With psychiatry as his specialty, he fulfilled his university training and considered consequent natural scientific methods and attitudes to be of critical value. In 1944 he broke his foot and suffered a heart attack. For a time he was very sick and his family thought he would die. What he experienced at the threshold of death he considered the most important experience of his lifetime, and he wrote about it in his book, *Memories, Dreams, Thoughts*, released in 1962 after his death.

    It was as if I found myself high up in space. Far below I saw the ball of Earth enwrapped in a wonderful, blue light. I saw the deep blue oceans and the continents. On many parts of the globe the Earth had dark green stains like oxidized silver. I knew I was about to move away from the Earth. Then something appeared in my vision. Close to me I saw a very dark clump of stones flying through the universe as I also flew through the universe. An entrance led to a little hall. To the right sat a dark Indian in the lotus position on a stone bench. He had on a white suit and rested completely still. He waited for me, silently. Two steps led into the hall and on the left side within the door stood the temple. There were numerous bowls filled with coconut oil and burning wicks that surrounded a door in the shape of a reef of burning flames. As I approached the steps to the entrance towards the cliffs, something uncommon occurred: I had the feeling that everything that had been in my life glanced off me. Everything I meant, wished for or thought about, the whole Earth's fantasticalness fell away or was stolen from me, an extremely painful experience. But something remained. It was as if everything I had ever experienced, everything that had happened around me was now with me. I could say: That was with me, and that was I. I consisted of that. I consisted of my history, and I had the feeling that it was I. "I am now that bundle of everything that was." This feeling gave me a feeling of complete emptiness but also great satisfaction.

    As I approached the temple, I was sure I would enter an enlightened room and meet everyone I truly belonged to. I was also sure I would understand the historical situation to which my life and I belonged. I would learn what was before me, how I was created, and where my life would continue to flow. My life appeared to me as a historical page upon which the text before and after was missing. My life seemed to be cut out of a long, continuous chain with many questions unanswered. Why did that happen? Why did I bring these prerequisites with me? What have I done with them? What will the consequences be? I wanted answers to all of these questions as soon as I entered the temple. I wanted to know why everything turned out the way it did and not differently. I wanted to find the people who could answer my questions about what had happened before and what will happen in the future.

    As I thought about these questions, something happened that caught my attention; below, from Europe rose an image. It was my doctor, or more correctly, a picture of him with a laurel wreath. I knew immediately it was the archetype of my doctor, Basilius from Kos [*basilius* means *king*, and Kos was the birthplace of the doctor Hippocrates and was famous for its Asclepiads temple]. A telepathic experience took place between us. He was sent to protest that I went away. I was very disappointed because everything seemed for nothing. I was not allowed to enter the temple and find the people who belonged to me. I must enter the "coffin system again." It was as if I built up an artificial three-dimensional world where every single person sat alone in a coffin. And now I tried to convince myself that this is meaningful. Life and the whole world seemed to be a prison, and I was irritated by the fact that I would soon learn that all of this was in beautiful order. I had been weightless and now it should once again end.

Just as Jung saw the doctor, it became clear that the doctor would soon die. Indeed, that did happen a few weeks later. Subsequently, one huge experience after another followed for Jung, much like the ones referred to above. The "experiences were absolutely real. Nothing was forced, everything had total objectivity." Here we see the spirit of the East, the Eastern experience of the world, appearing strongly in a Western person at the threshold of death.

Jung experienced everything within his under-conscious. It appeared non-stop from childhood and followed him through his whole life until the climatic moment on the threshold of death. He struggled constantly: How can I find security? How can I obtain a clear understanding of my experiences? How can I find my own individual existence within this enormous threshold that appears in full objectivity? Time after time he knew something would happen and it did. Something penetrated into Jung's three-dimensional field, bringing experiences of time in the past, present and future as a unified, objective totality.

Especially strong experiences of objectivity appeared when his wife died:

There I saw her in a dream. She stood at a little distance and looked at me. Her expression did not show happiness or sorrow, but objective understanding and knowledge without the slightest reaction of feelings. I knew it was not her real self but an image that was presented by her for me. It contained the beginning of our relationship and everything that had happened in our marriage of thirty-five years, as well as the end of her life. In relation to such a totality we remained silent for we could barely understand it.

The objectivity that I experienced in that dream and in the visions belongs to my completed individuation process. It entailed liberation from all value judgments and from all relationships in feelings. The pure feeling relationships normally include a lot to people but they always contain subjective projections, and this must be held back in order to arrive at yourself and to objectivity. The relationships of feelings are relationships of desire and are loaded with force and lack of freedom. Objective knowledge remains behind the relationships of feeling. That seems to be a central secret. Once we go through it a genuine unification (*conjunctio*) is possible.

What does Jung mean by *individuation*? It is a process that brings forth individuality, an undividable unity, and a totality. It entails becoming a single being. With individuality we mean our innermost, ultimate and true Self. "Individuation does not lock out the world but embraces it." Everything we sense and experience, everything that happens during our life, all of the people we meet belong to our Self. If we want to lock out something in our life, or if we pretend it does not belong to us, we remain in a limited, subjective consciousness. This includes everything we experience in the "outer" world as well as everything that appears in our "inner" world. When we discuss our Self, both our outer and inner lives melt together in one entity. The following words from Jung reflect not merely theory but the result of a mature, individualized experience: "First after my illness I understood how important it is to say *yes* to my own fate. For then it is a *self*, that does not disappoint when something unexplainable happens. It is a *self* that endures, that tolerates the truth and is mature to meet the world and individual destiny."

Jung was a man who struggled. There is such an overwhelming richness of pictures that streamed through him, they often threatened to take him away. Many times he considered the human being's existence to be but a temporary illusion, like waves of foam on top of powerful waves that fall forward from the depth of the archetypal under-conscious. Many times he seems about to disappear into an ancient Chinese cloud of bliss. Many times he seemed resigned from the possibility of breaking through to true knowledge of the comprehensive, objective spiritual world where there is no difference between outer and inner, between Self and the world, between the powers of nature and morality. And once again something new would shake up his life. Time after time he was confronted with a spiritual reality that he did not understand but wanted to understand and his struggles would begin anew.

Does not the Western approach provide more security? Is it not more secure to lock out the entire world that appears in the inner life, to lock out the ocean of pictures where anything can happen and everything seems uncertain? Should we not consequently refer to our outer senses and combine the impressions using our reason? Is not that a certain and secure existence? I have to ask: Secure for what? Secure for the individual's existence? Will the individual's existence be more secure with one-sided and consequent interest for the outer world, for material conquest? Nothing could be more less the case. Wherever this rules, we find a one-sided anti-individual tendency. Wherever technical-commercialization rules, human beings are reduced to part of the masses, to standardized types, and their thoughts are colored by the tyranny of public opinion. The individual is then described as a coincidental product of inheritance and environment.

In their unique one-sidedness, Both the West and the East's idiosyncrasies act indirectly anti-individual. In different ways, both remove to the same degree the individual human's existence when they affect people and are not integrated for separate tasks. In our struggle, our search for knowledge within our situation in life, whether it is within a Western or an Eastern path, we find the human potential to grow as an individuality. And in this battle a transformation takes place. The degree to which we find the Western and Eastern forces in our own Self and can say *yes* to both is the degree to which these forces no longer overpower us, but become our own forces.

When one discovers these forces, a new world opens up. New experiences are available for the human Self. It does not matter what education one has, where one stands in life or where one works. Here there are no dogmas and no authorities. It is the pure, spiritual activity of the individual, human Self that contains eternity and unlimited potential and also what seems to be unimportant. This is where an individual can find his path in life.

Reincarnation and Pedagogy

by

Valentin Wember

Translated by Karin Di Giacomo

Reincarnation and *karma* are central concepts within Spiritual Scientific pedagogy. This observation holds true—individual teachers find the questions regarding reincarnation and karma to be of preeminent importance for their work. They do inquire into the past, present and future fate of their children. For them, this inquiry is part of their life and forcefully inspires their work. However, this is not true in all Colleges of Waldorf teachers.

In general, there are no direct contextual references to reincarnation and karma in the publicly known so-called Waldorf essentials: Block lessons, class teachers, no letter grade requirements, no class repetition, eurythmy lessons, foreign language instruction starting in first grade, and strong emphasis on artistic subjects and methods. These so-called essentials can be and are indeed manifested without any background reference to reincarnation and karma. This is also due to the fact that more and more teachers at Waldorf schools no longer see themselves as anthroposophists or hold rather hesitant and skeptical views of anthroposophy. That does not prevent them from considering as meaningful and desirable the essential principles listed above or from using them as guidelines for their work.

The International Waldorf Teachers' Conference offered "Reincarnation" as the lead topic for the first time in 1996. During the preparation and follow-up phases of this convention, many schools worldwide dealt with this theme in pedagogical conferences. In this context I witnessed a colleague posing a question that contributed much to awakening an awareness of this issue: "What would change for us if we didn't have in the background these ideas of reincarnation and karma?" The answer was quite unequivocal: Not much! The developments outlined above shed light on the cause: If every teacher would evaluate and inquire personally how big a role the issues of reincarnation and karma played in his daily pedagogic work over the last five, ten or twenty years, a large majority of teachers would answer: This role was relatively small. Nearly everything we do in our daily work with the children not only *could* occur without any direct reference to these ideas, but it *did* and *does* indeed manifest without them.

And yet, this view is one-sided and distorting; it inadequately reflects the actual educational practices. This has to do with the fact that the entire system of Waldorf pedagogy is in essence based on a view of the human being in which reincarnation and karma are central facts. More precisely: Waldorf education is at its core based on an understanding of the human being, and this understanding developed experientially through "spiritual science" research, takes reincarnation and karma as empirical facts and not as faith-based concepts or results of visionary insights.

Consciousness-Based, Experiential Facts, Not Faith-Based Concepts
In the anthroposophical path of spiritual, consciousness-based, science intensified thinking, Rudolf Steiner described this path frequently. It is extraordinarily complex and has to be illumined from varying angles time and again. In this article I will limit myself to *one* aspect as described by Steiner.

The meditative concentration of thinking aims first at becoming self-aware of being engaged in this process. Normally we *have* thoughts. They occur to us. However this *occurring* is not the result of our own conscious efforts. We can create conditions conducive to thoughts occurring to us. But the *occurring* is not our own conscious doing. Therefore, when we observe the process with precision, we cannot say "I think" but in the moment of occurring, "it" thinks. The same is true for the stream of associations and imaginations that—as we say—go through our mind all day long. They *go through our mind*; that means we do not think them consciously.

When concentrating our thinking through meditation, it is important that we actually start to think on our own. We concentrate our thoughts on one object and keep focusing them on this point, so that the process of thinking indeed always originates in us.

> Originating from independent inner activity we must center our soul life on a topic (e.g. construct a symbol in front of our inner eye) and then limit our awareness entirely to this topic. We need to spend only few minutes on the topic of each practice session, because generally the length of time spent is irrelevant. More important is our ability to concentrate the soul's power toward one single point, which empowers and strengthens it from within. Then the inner faculty of thinking does not stay unnoticed, but is accompanied by such force that we sense it within and can experience it in our inner life. If we engage in such a soul experiment again and again with patience, perseverance and energy, we will finally experience how that otherwise elusive process of inner thinking truly arises in front of our soul.[1]

> We can also describe this same process with other words: "It is essential that the soul be compelled to bring forth much stronger forces from its own depth through concentration on a pertinent topic or image, forces that it is not required to draw on in ordinary life or in common understanding. The soul's inner agility is heightened by this process. The soul thus experiences itself in its true inner and independent essence."[2] This process of meditation contains additional steps which also can only be reached through persevering practice.[3]

Next we must acquire the faculty of completely releasing these images from consciousness and if we remain in naked (*empty*) awareness after the created images disappear, new and spontaneous "images arise, inspired by a realm beyond the world of the senses. We then enter that world which lies beyond the realm of the senses." We then first experience a tableau of our earthly life hitherto, back to approximately the moment of our birth. That emerges in front of our soul, not as a simple memory but as an immediate presence, all at once, so-to-say, as a time-organism which is mobile within itself. [4]

The soul reaches the next stage of cognition, if we manage to likewise suppress this living memory tableau by increasing the very forces that we previously used to suppress the self-created images. This is the stage when the world of spirit and soul forces is revealed which we traversed before birth or, let us say, before conception, the spiritual world of the soul in which we were immersed before descending into earthly existence, this world we carry within throughout our life on earth. This world lives in us, but in a manner like hydrogen is intermingled with oxygen in water.[5] Just as we cannot simply explore the hydrogen bound in water, we also cannot examine the inner realm of spiritual soul forces in our ordinary earthly existence. Only when we are transported into pre-life existence by the means described above, can we embark on such exploration. We have to "bring something into this world of spirit and soul forces that does not originate in the abstract world of thinking. We have to bring into it the devotion to the object. In the world of soul and spirit, we cannot truly and fully come to know a being or a force unless we fully extend our own being in love, unless we let ourselves surrender and fully enter into that which the inspiration presents. As we thus experience the reality of the spirit and soul forces in a living, exalted way, we are fully immersed in the intuitive realm."[6]

After returning from the experience of the world of soul and spirit forces, we now immerse ourselves in contemplating the collaboration between the corporeal-physical human being and the human being-ness (*essence*), which can only be experienced transcendentally. Such contemplation will allow us to understand the entire, complete human being. Pouring our awareness into that which transcendental cognition reveals, we also come to know the child, the human "becoming," in such a way that we can deal with him/her appropriately through the art of education and pedagogy.

Yet this path to realization as described above leads us further. The soul's life before earthly existence is not a uniform state, but a path traversing vast spaces and time spans.[7] The "spiritual scientist" can step-by-step pursue this path backwards—up to the threshold of physical death which was the gate to life on the plane of the spiritual and soul forces. Beyond that threshold the previous (last) earthly life becomes accessible and open to exploration. Only if we can trace the path of the soul to its previous incarnation can we be sure that we are dealing with one and the same soul in this life and the previous one—be it one's own or the soul of another human being. The opportunities for realization can, in the course of extended studies, include other souls and their pre-history. "The concept of *reincarnation*, meaning repeated lives on earth, now becomes a real observation. Experience gained regarding the inner core of the human life shows, so-to-say, the mutual imbedded-ness of human personalities, which stand in correspondence to each other. We can perceive these personalities only in a sequential time relationship—before and after. One incarnation always proves to be the result of a previous one." And the earthly lives that follow one after the other are "divided by interim periods of purely spiritual existence." This results in "the spiritual vision of existential forms that extend sequentially into the past."[8]

The method of realization outlined above describes the research method of Spiritual Science according to Steiner. All other images that arise in the soul and may be interpreted as memories of previous incarnations are unclear in their origin. They certainly can also arise from the physical organization of the human being, but these images are precisely not reflective of a person's permanent Self which exists beyond the body. The educational methods of Waldorf pedagogy are based on an understanding of the human being rooted in the research methods of Spiritual Science. They are based on an understanding of the human being as an individual spiritual entity who passes through repeated earthly lives. This matter is a fact only for the Spiritual Scientist and those students of Spiritual Science who have gone through such an experience independently and personally. There is no [conventional] proof for this hypothesis, but the steps on this path of realization can be rationally retraced and the manifold results of Spiritual Scientific research can be examined in regard to their inner coherence and congruence and compared with facts won through sensory experience. The educational methods of Waldorf schools are based on these results, and if applied wisely they can become heuristic working hypotheses which prove fruitful in practical education.

Reincarnation and Karma and the Methods of Waldorf Education

To begin with, an awareness of reincarnation and karma fosters and demands several basic pedagogic attitudes. Each teacher knows that the eternal essence of the student is inviolate. This essence can also not be "educated" by the teacher. Rather all education can in the final analysis only aim at raising the child towards a progressive unfoldment of his/her inner essence. Pedagogy as a whole is targeting the instrument—body and soul—of the incarnating being, and it has the high mandate of helping harmonize the two. For example, the teacher will take care not to confuse the temperament of a child with his/her essence. The individuality of the child is beyond the coloring of a temperament. In the spiritual world individuals are neither choleric nor phlegmatic. But individual beings embody in very specific constitutions in regard to the temperaments. Each temperament has its positive potentials and its perils. The decisive issue here is whether the temperament governs the human being or whether the human being can guide his/her temperament. Does the individual being master its instrument (the temperament), or is it oppressed thereby?

Each temperament that is ungoverned and overpowering is a special form of self-centeredness and egotism. All temperaments are specific forms of respective egocentric principles. But the ego is not the eternal being, not the eternal individuality. The temperaments are so-to-say a coloring hue of the ego. Ungoverned temperaments represent a panopticum of self-centeredness, none better or worse than the other. The very task of pedagogy is to take care that the temperament will not cover or hamper the individuality of the student, but that it becomes available to him/her in a healthy way. If the teacher so employs these methods to help the student even out his/her temperament and to govern it, he knows that he is rendering a service to the student's eternal individual being, which passes through repeated earthly lives and wants to make use of the temperament like an instrument.

The connection with previous lives on earth becomes even more tangible if the teacher realizes, within the context of Steiner's scientific findings, that the formative powers building the child's body are rooted in former lives, while the musical and language-oriented powers are a sort of seedling which will only unfold in the future. If the teacher works in this context on the language faculties of the child, he is a supportive collaborator in forming the child's future. Being aware of this role, the teacher can come into a heightened awareness of the significance and results of his efforts.

These two sketchy examples shall suffice here. They show the connections between the facts of reincarnation and karma and the daily practice of Waldorf pedagogy. Of course, these pedagogical approaches and methods can be applied without the conviction that reincarnation and karma are facts, but they would lose their true causative interrelationship. Many people who think about reincarnation and karma today find the relationships outlined here way too general. They probe deeper: What do these general concepts have to do with the supposedly specific previous lives of specific students? Do these specific relationships hold practical significance in Waldorf pedagogy? With these and similar questions, we are entering precarious territory.

In recent years a number of experiential accounts have been published outside the sphere of anthroposophy—and lately also within that circle—about specific memories of previous lives. Mostly, these are reports answering the question: Who was I in previous incarnations? In Waldorf pedagogy such questions have so far played a negligible role, just as have the questions: Who was this or that student in a previous life? What did (s)he experience that resulted in his/her current behavior, or having certain difficulties or talents? These questions have so far been rather irrelevant, because most teachers have a certain moral sense of tact, which has prevented them from speculating about these questions. Although this attitude has sometimes been called spiritually passive, I believe this is an unjust label. But that requires a more detailed explanation.

Are we allowed to speculate about previous incarnations of a student?

It is rude to speculate about the private life of an acquaintance or a friend. The private sphere of a person is not the concern of other people—and that is even truer for their intimate sphere. Trying to intrude into this sphere evidences pushiness and a lack of tact and constitutes a form of pollution of the human soul domain. It does not improve—and even exacerbates—the situation. This kind of intrusion has become "normal" behavior in these days, when we feed voyeuristic audiences with details from the private lives of numerous public figures. Compared with the intimate sphere, the previous incarnations of an individual are significantly more intimate than we can imagine. Any sense of respect for the dignity of another person should indeed bar us from engaging in such speculation. But those who do not share in such respectful sensitivities will find nothing to prevent them from speculating about previous fates of another human being. On the other hand it is remarkable that Steiner allows for an exception, precisely where an educator is concerned; he makes room for a gentle speculation about the previous fate of a child. However, this is indeed an exception and depends on essential and crucial conditions.

Steiner bases his exception on the assumption of karmic laws, that soul properties that become solidly habitual during a lifetime impact the individual soul and compel it to follow certain rules when building the physical body during its next incarnation. In other words, the properties of the soul become the architects of future physical bodies. If someone is for example a habitual liar, this characteristic will imprint itself upon the physical body of the next incarnation. What was a soul property in one life, e.g. a constant deformation of truth, will appear as a physical characteristic in the next incarnation. For example, now a person is no longer able to grasp the truth and becomes mentally retarded.[9] The transformation of habitual lying first into timidity and then to mental retardation in the next life is a spiritual law that the spiritual scientist Rudolf Steiner discovered. May an educator who has not himself explored this spiritual law, but knows it as a result of studying spiritual science research, speculate that a mentally retarded child was a habitual liar in a previous life?

Steiner answers this question in the affirmative, but he demands that at the same time moral conditions must be met. First, the educator has to participate speculatively in this fate of the child. He should imagine that it was (s)he who had been lied to in that former life. Secondly the educator has to derive a moral path of action from this speculation, forgive the child, and "meet the transgression with the best the educator has to give." The quote from Steiner reads: "There [with a retarded child] we have to imagine that we were those people who were often lied to by such a human being, and we should reciprocate the ill that we received from that person with the best we ourselves have to give. We must try to teach such a person a lot of the truths of spiritual life, and then we will see him or her blossom."[10] These remarks clarify the only rationale for a speculative consideration of previous lives: To help conceive of new moral-pedagogical ideas which lead to new pedagogical measures.

Mere speculation is of no use at all, and furthermore is rather destructive. At the same time Steiner's explanations illustrate how the moral consideration of reincarnation and fate can imbue pedagogy with new, unimagined resources, which would probably never have occurred to us without the concept of reincarnation. For this reason, Steiner's second example of these interrelations shall be introduced here as well. It deals with the karmic relationship between envy and a weak bodily constitution. In this regard, too, a soul characteristic shows only soul-related effects during a present lifetime. The envious person turns grouchy in old age and, often unable to care for him/herself, becomes dependent on others. But in the next incarnation, this soul-based habit manifests in the physical body:

> The weakness of the soul, engendered by envy in a previous incarnation, cannot really destroy the body that was built before the habit arose. But after we pass through the gates of death and come back for the next incarnation, these forces cause an organismic weakness in the energies that build the physical body. We can observe how a weak body is being built by such a person, who was so envious … in a previous incarnation.… As we think about a child that was born with a weak body into a certain environment, we not only have to realize these inner dynamics of karma, but we also come to a recognition that we are led to encounter human beings for certain reasons—not coincidentally. When a weak-bodied child has been born into a certain environment, we should ask ourselves: How should we act in regard to this issue? The correct behavior is always to take the highest moral road—to forgive. That will yield the best results here as well, and it constitutes the best education for that respective human being. Loving forgiveness towards a weak child, born into our life circle, engenders tremendous developmental effects. As we become strong transmitters for such forgiveness, we will see, how the child becomes stronger and stronger. If forgiving love resonates deep into our thinking, it will allow the child to gather the powers to reshape his/her former karma and come into a correct alignment. The child will also become physically strong.

The aim of all karmic insight points towards the future. Karmic insight in and of itself is useless and unproductive. The important goal is to set new, healing impulses through karmic insights. The poet and philosopher G.E. Lessing gave a very general expression to the thoughts contained in such considerations "The worth of a human being is not defined by the truth he or she owns or believes to own, but it is defined by the earnest effort expended to attain such truth. Because not in owning a truth but in exploring the truth, do expand our powers and this should be the measure of our ever-growing perfection. Ownership makes us dispassionate, inert and proud."

The worth of an educator does not lie in an *ownership* of a karmic memory which he thinks he has gained. Such worth is determined rather by the earnest effort (s)he expended in distilling new moral-pedagogical motives from such memories and by the strength of heart that led him/her to transform these motives into concrete actions.

Relying on a fundamental law that Steiner published in his *Knowledge of the Higher World and Its Attainment*, we can say: If any explorations of reincarnation and karma should *not* result in expanding my faculties of compassion, empathy and action from a ground of deep love, it deadens a power within me and threatens to lead me onto a dark path. Every exploration of karma and reincarnation that furthers us on our path towards sincere compassion and active love also guides us on the path of light and realization (*enlightenment*) and towards the radiance (*warmth*) of the power of sacrifice.

Endnotes
1. Steiner, Rudolf. "The eternal powers of the human soul," lecture, Berlin, December 3, 1915; in R. Steiner, *About the Spiritual Life of Central Europe*, GA 65, Dornach, 2000, p. 63f.
2. Steiner, Rudolf. *An Outline of Occult Science* (1st edition 1910), GA 13, Dornach, 1989, p. 318.
3. The following text along the lines of R. Steiner, "The Healthy Development of the Human Being," lecture, Dornach, December 26–27, 1921, GA 303, Dornach, 1987, pp. 73–94.
4. Ibid.
5. Detailed presentation by R. Steiner in *Theosophy* (1st edition 1904), GA 9, Dornach, 2002, pp. 90–157.
6. This paragraph along the lines of R. Steiner, "The Psychological Foundations and Epistemological Positioning of Anthroposophy," lecture, Bologna, April 8, 1911; in *Philosophy and Anthroposophy*, GA 35, Dornach, 1984, p. 133 f.
7. Steiner, Rudolf. Lecture of November 26, 1910, in *Pathways and Objectives of the Spiritual Human Being*, GA 125, Dornach, 1992.
8. Ibid.
9. Ibid.

About the author:
Valentin Wember was born in 1957. He attended the Free Waldorf School in Krefeld. He studied literature, philosophy, history, music and pedagogy in Hamburg, Berlin and Stuttgart, and earned his PhD in 1984. Since 1985, he has been a high school teacher for German and history at the Michael Bauer School, Stuttgart. He has been active in various Teacher Training Institutes in Germany, Switzerland, Ukraine and the USA, and has worked as an organizational consultant.

Moral Imagination

by

Oscar Borgman Hansen

translated by Ted Warren

What should be the dominant feeling in modern man? Living in a highly civilized country and reviewing one's personal life, the immediate answer must be a feeling of thankfulness. We all have reason to experience an active, deep and lively feeling of thankfulness for living in a society where distress is unknown for most people, where we are helped medically and socially during illness, where law presides and there are no foreign restraints, and where there is time and money to experience art and literature, enjoy sports or travel abroad. And if we look beyond the accidents that our destiny may bring our way or the difficulties each individual faces; all dissatisfaction must be transformed to concern of an impersonal nature, a concern for the thoughtlessness with which these goods are enjoyed, a concern for the future of mankind. Yet we seldom experience this feeling of thankfulness, instead more often the feeling of dissatisfaction.

Emptiness in the midst of abundance seems more common than sustainable joy. The feeling of emptiness is accompanied by another feeling, the feeling of powerlessness in relation to the overwhelming, global political game that seems to demote human beings to a passive, observer mentality. There is no way to take action. We do not act, we are acted upon. And once we have accepted biology as the most fundamental aspect of human life, we become observers of our own willpower, we allow ourselves to float on a sea of desires and no longer believe we have a power in us that can calm the storm. These feelings, so prevalent today, were not so widespread in earlier times. Therefore we experience them as unnatural. It is difficult to capture in concepts the feelings of emptiness without using irrelevant generalizations and abstract thoughts. Nevertheless I will attempt to say something meaningful about this situation. For if the feelings of emptiness are to be overcome and transformed, they must first be understood.

If a person is convinced that he has the power to solve a certain issue, his confidence can strengthen his power to do just that. If a person is convinced he is helpless, he will not solve the issues, for human beings create themselves out of the thoughts they make about themselves. And to people's thoughts today belong the ideas that (1) they are products of inheritance and environment and that (2) their actions are determined by natural and social needs. Such convictions are part of the reason why people's inner activities are paralyzed. If one believes that his most important needs will be satisfied by a well-being in the physical world, that conviction will contribute to one's emptiness, even when prosperity grows. For it is not the outer conditions that make people satisfied, but rather the ability to transcend sensory impressions, to stand independently in life and create the possibilities to obtain inner riches that become more and more independent from outer conditions. That a person can overcome himself is part of being human. Knowing that our biological needs are not most important but that we create in ourselves a purer, refined form of the human being can give us security in life and replace the emptiness and dissatisfaction with our inner life. Too many people have forgotten Solomon's wise words: It is greater to steer your consciousness than take a city.

To the most important tasks we have today belong the abilities to find the right motives in our willpower and to put these motives into action. For it is not enough to have the right motives, "to want to do the right thing." Just because one wants to do the right thing, it is not certain that one knows how. To accomplish something certain one must move beyond. Many people act with "good will" and create catastrophes or results that are directly the opposite of what they intended. Yet their motives were right. A politician wants peace but he is forced to create war—in the name of peace. To transcend that paradox it is not enough to say that one must consider concerns that are more important than peace, even if that can be true. Possibly his wish for peace was genuine. Parents who want to be more confidential with their children can find themselves pushing their children farther away. The well-intended person may facilitate conflict resolution and wind up messing things up beyond redemption. Or the CEO who wants to lead his company for the company's and the employees' best may become bitter when he realizes he is not mature enough to do so. Instead, he who has achieved a good position in society and has everything he wants now spends his evenings in front of the television experiencing that life is becoming more and more empty.

With these examples I do not want to say that this is the way life is, but rather, that life is *also* like this. I am illustrating the problem of finding the way from the right motive, that which the person has unconditionally made his own, to the realization of that motive in life! This path follows the course Rudolf Steiner termed *moral imagination* and *moral technique*. He understood moral technique to be the knowledge and know-how that is necessary to realize a certain moral goal, knowledge and know-how that can be learned. It is the technique to master the way to reach the goal in real life. The concept of moral imagination is of utmost importance. With it we realize that is not the mistakes in life that prevent us from finding the way to realizing our motives, but the fact that we have not found the creative forces in our being.

With imagination we can create mental images that relate to something other than what already exists. The process involved in imagination is distinguished from the process of thinking in that thinking works with concepts while imagination works with mental images. Concepts are always generalizations, generalizations that include a number of separate ones that are shared in common and together create a certain type. Mental images on the other hand are concrete, for example a memory of my grandmother's chair in contrast to the concept "chair" that contains everything in common with all chairs.

Another example: Given the word "triangle," I see with my inner eye a black one on a white background; it can have pointed angles or right angles but it must have a certain size. The concept "triangle" does not have these concrete characteristics. When I think of a concept I think of that which is in common to all triangles, i.e., the laws of triangles; for example the sum of three angles in a triangle is 180 degrees—for every triangle no matter what the shape may be.

If we think of the concept "school," we have a building for educating children, whether or not it is built of bricks with large windows and broad steps. The mental images in our memory recall that which we saw, heard or experienced with other senses at an earlier time. To the contrary we create mental images from imagination without recreating outer reality, yet the images have the same concrete characteristic as mental images from memory.

Steiner defined "mental image" as an individualized concept while most philosophers and psychologists who have worked with the relationship between concept and mental images consider concepts to be generalizations. Behind that technical/philosophical distinction lies a difference in perception that is of the utmost importance. If you consider concepts to be generalized mental images, then in our thinking we bring forth abstractions from reality that is of a sensory and physical nature. Thinking represents and compares the outer reality and brings forth that which many individuals have in common. If, to the contrary, a mental image is an individualized concept, it encompasses reality beyond our senses and thereby reaches our thinking through activity not with a passive representation. This is exactly what Steiner proved so convincingly: The content of a concept is not a representation of a diluted sensory experience but it appears in our consciousness as something independent within in our thinking, and this is a spiritual reality. This is not a subjective function, but a spiritual force that is common to all human beings.

Mankind's moral ideals must be expressed in the form of concepts. They have a general character: to do the good, to work for peace, for justice, for progress. Such ideals can be made concrete to a certain degree, yet they continually retain the characteristics of a concept. For example, someone views the progress in a certain political party's program to be good because it includes his religion and he considers the settlement of differences in wealth between the developed countries and the industrialized countries as the most important demand for justice in our times. With this concept of a political program with a certain religion and with justice for developing countries, we are led to a specific existence but so general that we have not yet understood anything concrete. Yet if we work for a moral ideal, we must know how to do it concretely: we have to find our place within the political party, within the congregation and in the work for developing countries. If we do not find the concrete relationship, our work is impossible.

The feeling of helplessness occurs when we know what we want to do, when the wish or the willpower is present, but we do not find our way to the concrete fulfillment: How can I fulfill my good will? This question may go unanswered. One path to the concrete may entail allowing others to tell one what he should do. If an individual is in a community that he trusts, he will be happy to take the place others have found for him. Knowing there is a need for him fills him with purpose and satisfaction. If one does not have such a community, he does not have such help. Yet for those who have supportive communities and those who do not, both have the possibility to search for moral imagination.

With imagination we mean the ability to create mental images that do not relate to something other than what already exists. We find imagination at work in our daydreams, our private stories, pictures of the future and wishful thinking. In all of these instances we create pictures of something that contains certain aspects of reality but does not necessarily exist. And this occurs with no obligation to reality.

In *artistic imagination* we have, to the contrary, a form of imagination that has laws, an imagination that leads to something, that awakens certain impressions of beauty. Whoever enjoys works of art shall have exact experiences or feelings presented: a result of the work of imagination—telling a compelling story, finding the convincing picture in a lyrical poem, composing a melody, or placing motifs together in a painting in such a way that no one else has previously done. Every good artist must master his imagination so that his works are created. Artists must submit their imagination to the artistic discipline.

In *Philosophy of Freedom* Steiner put forth the concept of moral imagination. With this concept he demonstrated that whoever wishes to realize a moral goal must be able to generate the mental images through which these goals may be set into real life. It is not enough to have the will to work with an idea if there are not people who can tell you how to do it. If these people do not exist, one must use his imagination to create the mental images that individualize the ideas and mental images that pertain to them and also to present them in concrete examples. The general concept or ideal of working with justice must be individualized, into concrete mental images concerning relevant work for justice. And with human actions it depends on realizing that which has not existed previously with the help of the individualized process of imagination. This imagination, much as the artistic imagination, must seek mental images that have not already existed but that can become reality. If one chooses to work with justice, then one must search for the situations in life where such work is needed and find one's own way to make it happen—as a writer, politician, lawyer or artist. There are thousands of possibilities but it is up to the individual or the group to find them.

The person who lacks moral imagination may have moral ideals but they will remain abstractions. He may preach morality but in order to create something new, he will have to inspire other people to bring it into the deed.

Artistic work has great importance in education, not only because it provides certain experiences, but also because it helps awaken the creative forces that strengthen the child's imagination. Two things are necessary for anyone who will be a creative member of society: a strong moral will and a lively moral imagination that can manifest into realities in the world.

Where do we find examples of moral imagination? Everywhere! In the ability to find the little, unexpected gift that spreads joy, to find the friendly or encouraging word, to release the resolving laughter. From all of these small things in life we move to the greatest matters and tasks to resolve difficult social, educational or political problems. To lead thousands of devastated prisoners from German prisons safely to Sweden during the final days of World War II was a deed that displays willpower and courage and moral imagination. This brings us back around to the issue that life does not have to be empty, and we do not have to feel helpless. If we use not only pure willpower but also moral imagination, we find possibilities everywhere. Then we can be truly free.

The Christmas Mystery and the Knowledge of Evil [1]

by

Dr. Hermann Poppelbaum

Even at Christmas, the most peaceful of the year's festivals, the contrasting voice of evil rumbles audibly and uncannily, seeking to assert its ancient connection with man. In the face of the most innocent and defenseless child, the powers of destruction draw together with their most relentless threats. Bethlehem is to become the site of the most execrable infanticide.

This image in itself should suffice to shake up modern man in his quest for the true meaning of the Christmas event. In the light of the consciousness soul, Christmas cannot be thought of without the impact of the evil forces which venture forth as closely as possible to innocence and there reach out ruthlessly for their blow. It is not their fault that this plot fails; the child (on its flight to Egypt) passes right through the enemies lying in wait for it—even as later on the Redeemer escapes, by passing right through the crowd of his pursuers. With impressive grandeur he says to his enemies: "Where I am, ye cannot go." Even as a child, Jesus is enveloped by this aura of unapproachableness, protecting him like a cloak.

Rudolf Steiner lifted a corner of the veil concealing the Christmas Mystery by assigning to the epoch of the consciousness soul the task of discovering the seat of evil in man. The mystery consists in the fact that evil is allotted the place it must have, namely as a counter-weight to the freedom of the human ego. Evil is a component of human nature, which is formed in such a way that it may attain freedom. In the wonderful structure "The Human Being" the gods achieved their greatest and most far-reaching deed, by assigning to the sworn antagonistic forces (and beings) a space wherein they can work in their own way without causing permanent harm. Spiritual-scientific knowledge should learn to describe this space. How can it be found?

In primeval times, the forces adverse to man and hostile to the gods were allowed to manifest themselves only in the instructive image of the myth. The direct relationship of the deformed shapes of evil with the image of man could be divined only faintly and shudderingly, but it could not be grasped concretely. Even the Sphinx, after she had solved the riddle, cast herself into the abyss still concealed to man. Only the initiate Oedipus was allowed to see the abyss yawning in the human being.

The modern science of initiation brings us still closer to the focus of these destructive forces. Man may ignore their existence for a time, to the detriment of his self-knowledge, whereas Steiner's help in the search for knowledge casts a bright, indeed a comforting light into the abyss.

According to Steiner's description, evil is chiefly connected with the protracted activity of forces which go on working even though their time has run out. This is a characteristic that may be used as a real distinctive mark in the search for evil. For example, evil arises when hereditary forces go on working after they have lost their carrying power and yet refuse to withdraw. They must be replaced by entirely different forces, so that they may not disrupt the course of evolution.[2]

Another example is the protraction of the influences going out from the cultural life of nations, although the time has come in which the Christ-impulse must replace them. These are forces which persist in their work, have an Old Testament character, and represent the retarded part of the influence going out from the Elohim, a part which has remained behind and is connected with the Moon.[3]

In Steiner's *Letters on the Michael Mystery* we read that forces which persist in forming man in a wrong direction should be rejected and replaced by the forces of Michael who follows the Christ. The path of least resistance, the linear continuation, as it were, leads to evil. If, after being born, the human being continues to submit to the forces which have formed him until birth, he will become sinful.[4] Original sin derives its name from this. It arises because these forces have refused to transform themselves. It is not Nature that is sinful, as the Archbishop wrongly asserts in Goethe's *Faust,* but the forces which man takes over unchanged, predispose him to "sinfulness." The affirmation of Nature, so frequently encouraged in the present time and considered as a healing element, can therefore lead to misfortune, to disaster. The indispensable thing which the human being needs more than anything else, is the novel constituent in him. This is neither hereditary nor can it be transmitted by heredity.

In the story of Christ, the "holy pair" *(das hochheilige Paar)* does not see in *Jesus* the child to whom it has given birth, but sees in him the Heavenly Child. The *Oberufer Play* dispels the illusion that Joseph is the Child's father by bringing in the delightful note (Steiner draws attention to it) of a very old Joseph, already in a slightly doddering state. The spiritual origin of the Christ Child, from the womb of the Cosmic Mother, thus gains the upper hand. The seam of her garment is merely touched by the earthly element, which casts its folds. But evil remains under her feet and will draw nigh at a later stage.

The beasts at the manger indicate the path leading into the animal realm, beginning outside the sphere of the covering cloak, leading to the animal which does not yet appear in the grotesque aspect filling man with horror. The beasts at the manger, ox and donkey, are innocent images of the not-yet human. They are indications pointing to the center of evil, but have not yet arisen from evil. Within the human being evil developed as a separate center, and from there it sets "the whole world afire," as Steffen expresses in his poem *Die Jüngerin.*

Steiner was able to show that especially the kernel of the human being's existence rests upon a predisposition to destruction working in the human organism as such and giving the ego its earthly consciousness—the shadow, as it were, against which the ego's contours can be set off. This description of a physiological-spiritual structure derived from spiritual vision should not be confused with a theory of evil. When the zoologist Konrad Lorenz speaks of the animal's aggressive instinct as the archetype of evil latent in man, he does not describe a fact which he observed, but an abstractly construed transposition without any genuine transformations. The instinct remains unchanged and is merely covered up by social habits.[5] In Steiner's description we have a material process working destructively in the human organs, serving as a reflecting surface (a mirroring device) for the ego's consciousness. When the destructive process breaks through into the half-conscious soul-region, the result will be an instinctive destructive urge. Instead of bodily substance which must be destroyed in order to awaken consciousness, the destructive element is thrown out into the environment, where it begins to spread. Evil arises only in the social sphere.

We should clearly grasp that evil in the social sphere is connected with the acquisition of the ego. Animals can therefore have no inner center of destruction as a force opposed to the development of the ego, but they consume their bodily substance as they grow old. Old animal-specimens begin to "fret," and at the same time segregate themselves from the herd. They do not transform themselves, but give back their spiritual part to the Group Soul.

What is wonderful in the human structure, however, is the fact that the above-mentioned center of evil is built into every individual as a useful element for the further development of the ego. From the imaginative aspect, not yet from the natural-scientific one, the myth presents evil as something existing from remote times and "still allowed to be there" by permission of the divine powers, e.g. as a preceding generation of gods, such as the Titans of ancient Greece who formed the foundation for Zeus' realm of light. There is as yet no insight into how the human ego may reach his portion of light through the fall of the Titans. The concept that light exists everywhere in darkness reveals itself only after Christ's descent into Hell. The journey to the nether world is no longer exclusively the concern of initiates, but has, so to speak, been forced upon every "bearer of the consciousness soul." He encounters evil not only as an image, but also as a fact reaching right into the bodily foundations of his existence. He sees what the ancients could not see—the physiological supports of his ego upon the earth. The "journey to the nether world," lit up by the light of Christ, becomes knowledge.

Modern man must learn to view evil as an unavoidable element of development, without which he could not develop himself. But only when the destructive tendency in man is turned, can the ego begin to ray out. The destructive instinct (Cain's weapon) lurking in the astral body is covered up by the Guardian, by the Angel with the Sword, but it is there nevertheless. This destructive instinct still seeks to call up the fight of all against all. It must be rerouted towards the sheaths of the human being, where it is no longer destructive but is blunted and produces images. Wherever man unfolds thoughts he has interrupted a Cain-deed.[6]

This is what man may know today, or what he may at least, divine. In this striving for knowledge, he is working at the dark background—hidden by the light of the Christmas event—which must nevertheless be there and be recognized.

Endnotes
1. Christmas Conference lecture given at the Goetheanum on the December 25, 1964.
2. From the cycle *In geänderter Zeitlage*, 5th lecture dated July 12, 1918.
3. Ibid., p. 97.
4. Lecture dated May 15, 1921.
5. Konrad Lorenz, *Das sogenannte Böse. Zur Naturgeschichte der Aggression*, 1964.
6. Rudolf Steiner, "Welche Bedeutung hat die okkulte Entwicklung des Menchen für seine Hülen und sein Selbst?" 8th lecture, The Hague, March 27, 1913.

Evil and the Well-Intended

by

Oscar Borgman Hansen

translated by Ted Warren

The problem of evil emerges dramatically in modern times; it quickly becomes terrible and seems impossible to resolve in a way that will satisfy the soul and the intellect. The problem of evil is a natural part of the entire moral dilemma. The way we perceive morality affects the way we perceive evil. Concerning morality we generally do not move beyond consequent subjectivity. The most consequent exposition is probably found in the logical empiricist's concept of all moral understanding as permanent, non-theoretical statements which are impossible to declare true or false—not because this lack is too difficult but because these statements lie beyond that which can be true or false. If someone declares that in Finmark there are human beings with wings, we can know whether or not that is true by sending an expedition to the distant forests of Northern Norway, and when the expedition returns to tell us there are no human beings with wings in that region, then the declaration is proven false. But how can one resolve a declaration such as: Women should have the same rights in society as men. Someone else can say: Women are created to be subservient to men and therefore the right to vote is absurd. Few will agree, but are majority and minority solid criteria for determining what is true or false? If that were so, the truth and the false would switch places, the logical empiricists solving the problem in their own way.

Moral declarations are to be understood as statements and statements are neither true nor false. One knows what is meant when someone says, "Coffee, ah!" or "Alcohol, usch!" But one cannot say that either person has made the right statement. Moral statements should be understood in the same way. For example, "Equal rights for women, fantastic!" or "Equal rights for women, No!"—we do not argue such statements but realize that opinions and tastes differ. Morality is nothing other than different peoples' or different societal groups' absolutely subjective ways of relating to human actions.

There are many people today who distance themselves from radical perspectives, not so much because the consequences are difficult to accept, but because they have nothing to replace them with. For example, in Danish public opinion debates, participants speak consequently about morality as an expression of "attitudes," attitudes, for example, that involve values and behavior. Yet attitudes are totally subjective even when you consider "socially acceptable or desirable attitudes." One does not move beyond the absolute subjectivity but is reluctant to admit it because it is so hard to live with.

And when we address the problem of evil, subjectivity must be out of the question. That the Nazis committed evil deeds cannot be just a matter of feeling equivalent to all other feelings; until the Nazis were defeated, it caused the defeat of such reactions. But if morality is subjective, what is the error in such arguments? In our time we do not seem ready for an intellectual resolution to evil and therefore we are not ready for a moral resolution to it.

In all ages the problem of evil has been a riddle. Let us we revisit the time of Greek philosophy and the first years of Christianity to see how evil was experienced then. We find a world-historic opposition between Socrates and St Paul in their understanding of evil. Socrates was certain that no one commits an evil act except through misunderstanding. No one wants evil. Evil hurts the one who commits it and no one wants to hurt himself. Who would create pain by cutting himself with a knife? Yet he who hurts himself by consuming too much alcohol hurts himself, although in a way that manifests only years later. And it is easy to say, "It will not go wrong!" Even more obvious are the amoral actions of theft and murder. Such actions cause serious injury to the person's soul. According to Socrates, if one were to understand the situation all the way from the deed through punishment and the consequences after death, one would stay away from evil.

In contrast to Socrates' convictions we have St Paul's position: Until I understand my own actions, I do not what I want but hate which I hate to do. When I do what I do not want to do, I act according to the law and thereby make sure the deed is good. Then it is no longer I who acts, but the sin that lives in me. Until I realize that in my flesh there lives nothing good, I have the will to do good, but I cannot carry out the good. The good I want to do I do not, but the evil I do not want, I do." (Rome. 7, 15–19) What St Paul expressed does not necessarily correlate to his Christian beliefs. The pagan Ovid expressed the same conviction with equally precise words, *Video meliora proboque, sed deteriora sequor.* "I see what is better and acknowledge it, but I do what is worse."

This essay is not intended to be a discussion on the meaning of evil. In modern times we measure evil within ourselves. The question is whether or not we can overcome evil in our souls. Socrates attributes insight as having enough power to overcome evil. St Paul thinks human beings can overcome evil only through grace.

Can modern people find an answer through observing these opposing convictions? Many will agree that St Paul: Who has not done that which he does not want to do, against his better insights, driven by some form of egoism? Many are familiar with the sin of procrastination: "I really should do that today, but there is no problem if I wait until tomorrow. I will wait, for I would like to finish reading this exciting book right now." The inner tendency to leave things undone or until later strengthens Socrates' viewpoint, in a wider sense with arguments that forgive the procrastination: "There is no problem if I delay until tomorrow." Perhaps the accident will occur anyway, but we cannot know in advance.

Characteristic of a lot of evil is that it occurs within something well-intended. Those who commit evil deeds do so because they want something they consider good, in other words, the ends justify the means. This is a very prevalent aspect of evil in today's world. Many consider themselves controlled by an evil, they acknowledge the evil. We want what we consider good, and when we act on it, we commit evil.

Bent Jensen, Danish scholar and historical scientist, published a very interesting book, *The Fascination with Stalinism*, in which he cites highly respected and good people who admired Stalinism and Communism for the social progress achieved in Russia, and who closed their eyes to all the cruelty, considering the reports of evil as exaggerated. Similarly many good and rational people accepted Nazism. Idealists in one place, idealists in another place, all very blind and with insufficient insight.

There may be no doubt that an individual's or a group's concept of good and evil relates to that individual's or group's world perspective. Those who believe that a nuclear defense is legitimate do so because it is their only defense against a powerful and evil enemy, the lesser of two evils. No doubt there are cynical people with no conscience who are ready to destroy whatever they hate. Yet cynical people are in the minority compared with those who apologize for accepting certain negative consequences of what they consider for the most part good. If we believe that class struggles are the basis for progress, we act differently than if we believe that progress is the result of peaceful activities. There is a difference in our understanding of reality, a difference in our cognition that creates differences in our understanding of good and evil in each particular situation. On the other hand we are in agreement about ideas; for example, we all want progress. But what is progress? That is the question of knowledge!

In ancient times and during the Middle Ages, it was common to identify the true and the good; one could say that the true and the good are the same. Another assumption was that there are different degrees of reality. Evil was something found in the world of artificial experience. It was something that really did not exist. God is that which summarizes the truly good and the complete reality. Therefore goodness is always judged according to the will of God.

Modern people who have embraced scientific development as truth do not judge goodness according to the will of God. They ask their own insight for advice and often end up in conflict because insights differ. If we concentrate on the basis of the conflict, we discover common ground that is often hidden or misconstrued. The groups who are fighting, willing to kill each other, are actually striving for the same goals, "progress and justice."

In *Philosophy of Freedom* Rudolf Steiner states that a conflict between two free individuals is impossible. He argues that free people act upon moral intuitions that appear in their thinking from a world of thinking accessible to all. Thinking surrounds us all with a common content. If we truly act from an intuition or an insight, we will understand our fellow human beings. Freedom creates the understanding. To be free we sacrifice duty. The free person does not do what he should do but what he wants to do. That which he wants to do has been discovered through the power of love in his thinking. This is actually the same true state of being, but this state of being can be lifted to a higher level of existence, from the ideal sphere to the level of existence where the idea's empirical subjectivity is overcome—by spiritual empiricism.

When Steiner published his second version of *Philosophy of Freedom*, he summarized his goal with this book in a lecture on October 27, 1918. He spoke about the scientific basis for the idea of freedom and added:

> I wanted to further develop the idea of freedom as a world concept, to show that only he can understand freedom and follow it in the right direction who senses that, in the inner life of man, there is something that not only appears in the purely earthly but also in the larger cosmic world processes that streams through mankind and can be understood in the inner life of a human being. And only when the larger cosmic world processes are experienced in the inner life of a human being, when they are enlivened in the inner, is it possible to reach a philosophy of freedom by understanding the inner life of man as something cosmic. He cannot reach a philosophy of freedom who wants to guide his thoughts by the outer sensory guidelines that have been pointed out by modern natural scientific education. This is a tragedy in our times—people at our universities all over the world are educated to guide their thoughts primarily by outer sensory impressions. Therefore we have entered an epoch where we are more or less helpless in relation to our ethical, social and political challenges. The thinking that merely allows one to enter the outer sensory experience will never be able to free itself in the inner man, to raise itself to intuitions that are necessary to reach if thinking shall unfold in human deeds. Therefore the impulse for freedom is closed out by thinking that is guided by modern scientific guidelines.[1]

From the understanding of freedom, the good is consolidated by reality and in this way only experienced by individually liberated, human thinking. If the liberation of thinking does not take place with natural science's *tugt*, we have unrestricted rather than liberated people.

If we understand freedom in this way, we can see that the capacity for evil has a mission in human development. For only through this tendency will we understand the task of developing ourselves as free human beings. Evil prevents us from being ourselves. As St Paul said: Evil is a power that lives in us. By overcoming it, we become free, and we become free by educating our thinking to be penetrated spiritually by the world cosmic processes. By liberating thinking, it becomes a power in us, it becomes willpower. "Willpower is the idea as power."[1] If we allow the idea to work in us as willpower, the inner liberation overcomes the tendency to evil, but liberation would never appear had not first the tendency for evil appeared as a seduction that springs from well-intended actions. This is the challenge, the battle to develop a greater awakening and thereby to liberate.

In this regard Socrates was right in his conviction that the relationship between insight and evil concerns the future goals of humanity, while St Paul's description talks to relationship in the present condition of mankind. Although it should be evident that the topic of evil has not been fully exposed in this article, the reader has now had the opportunity to review one aspect of evil.

Endnote
1. Steiner, Rudolf. *The Philosophy of Freedom*, London: Rudolf Steiner Press, 1964.

Craft and Morality

by

Dr. Thomas Weihs

From *The Cresset*, Vol. 14, No. 4

I have always known that there is an intimate connection between craft and morality. Everyone knows that in craftsmanship, in its activity and aura, something utterly moral is centered. But just why there is this connection is not easy to answer because morality has become a very problematic and exclusive concept.

I will try first to turn to the question of crafts and look at the problem from the point of view of history and of humankind. Then I would like to go into the question of morality and the connection between craft and morality and the individual.

It is difficult to find the first beginnings of craft. We know that it was at its height during the Middle Ages. But if one looks back into primeval times, one finds that craft did not exist separately, and it is probable that human creativity started as art and not craft. The more that becomes now known of primitive human activity, the more one sees that in the beginning of time, humans created artifacts, things they made with their own hands, for magical but not practical purposes. Probably the first dwellings were not built for men but for the gods to inhabit. Probably the first things were made in an attempt to communicate with divine beings and forces rather than to deal with the needs of earthly existence. We know countless paintings that are ten, fifteen, and twenty-thousand years old. We know sculptures of these times as well as articles of daily use. But as far as one can assess the early epochs of humankind, it seems that the physical material creations were, to begin with, of a religious and cultic nature and only gradually of a practical nature. This would seem to be an indication that craft may be a further step from art.

Among the very early artifacts of art or craft there are symbols, symbolic forms and shapes. One of the earliest and most frequent is the human hand. In some French and Spanish caves containing early paintings, hands are depicted in all kinds of positions. In some caves hundreds, thousands, of hands are painted: in others just one hand. Some walls are painted with abstract hand and finger forms. Not only in Europe but also in other countries of early times, one finds the symbol of the human hand. Other symbols of the early artistry of humankind are the female and male and the animal, but amongst these forms the hand seems to be the most widespread and possibly the oldest.

Some of you will know the German word for craft is *Handwerk*—a very apropos word because craft is bound to the hand. Only things made with the hand are objects of craft. The hand is the organ, the place, the origin, and even the meaning of craft. The hand is a unique organ and distinguishes the human being from all other kingdoms of nature. It is an organ that to begin with did not belong to the earth: it was originally an organ of sense and communication. It was not meant to work but to speak, to sense, and to experience the world. Thus craft might be seen as the result of a sacrifice on the part of the hand in giving itself to the needs of the earth.

In the earliest cultures of which we know—Sumer, Egypt, Ur—one can distinguish definite craftsmanship of the highest skill and achievement. We see in some of the magnificent Egyptian, Sumerian, and Chaldean sculptures and earthenware (in the British and other museums) how the hardest and most resistant of materials were shaped and formed to utmost perfection. Much was not done as works of art but as crafts.

What do we mean today when we refer to arts and crafts? These two concepts have changed and developed to some extent, and when I mention the old art and craft I use terms as we use them today. But we mean something different and the essential difference is this:

We have an object of craft when we know exactly what we wanted to make and proceeded to make it as exactly to our plan as possible. Therein lies the craft. For example, a cabinet maker may plan to make a table knowing exactly what it will be like, but if it turns out to be a bed, he is a bad craftsman. Equally if a man sets out to make an ashtray and makes it exactly as planned, he is not an artist but a good craftsman. The essence of art is that something new arises, not only materially according to a given plan or form, but that between the artist and a wide realm of influences something entirely new appears. It may be a work of art if the artist develops a new form. He may have it completely in his head, but if he has not developed it in connection with a particular material, again, he is no artist.

The craftsman wrestles for the expression of an existing entity, and it is the process of incarnation into material existence with which he deals. The artist wrestles for new form, new content that is to come about between himself and the world. It is probably through artistic endeavor that crafts have developed. But craft is a further step and enters into a sphere different from that of art.

I have already said that in ancient history craft existed in the sense of my attempt to separate it, somewhat artificially, from merely artistic activity. The task of art was the material incarnation of forces determined out of the human being's spiritual and religious life. The iconoclastic aspect of art is the craft aspect, which has played the greatest part throughout the history of mankind.

In our present day meaning, crafts reached their height and fulfillment in the Middle Ages. In it an interesting occupation played an astonishing part, and that was the work of the mason. In connection with building and a revival of primeval impulses of building not for the sake of shelter but for the sheltering of divinity, the houses of God, quite a phase in the development of craft began: the fact that one man can make an object with his hands out of material. Not an object assembled but one made from material by one man with his own hands. The great cathedrals of Europe were built in this way. One man carved a stone wanting it to be as perfect as possible and put it in place. They began to acquire perfection not as artists or sculptors wanting to bring about something new but wanting their handmade stone to be a worthy part of the House of God, which they were helping to build. That is the origin of the magnificent sculptures of Romanesque and Gothic churches all over Europe. And in other fields, too, this striving of one man to perfect his handiwork developed.

Schools were set up in which these skills were taught, not only physical skills but skills in spiritual knowledge. We will understand the development of craft life at that time if we think of another activity that was developing at the same time. Men's professions were varied: there were always hunters, soldiers, traders and those who rendered services, the carters, the barbers who were the surgeons and doctors, and the clergy. In medieval society the tendency to dissipate life was very marked not only amongst soldiers and traders but also amongst the clergy and generally what one calls morality was weakened and endangered. Within this society there were two groups of people who developed very earnest schools of moral training: the craft guilds and the alchemists.

The alchemists are remembered largely on the basis of misunderstanding. They were the scientists of that time who tried to study processes of nature as examples of the development of the human soul. What has been described and handed down as secret knowledge of the purification and transformation of base metals into gold was an attempt to train the individual human soul, to enable its base qualities by observing chemical processes in nature that seemed to illustrate processes of inner development. This was one attempt to improve the moral nature of the human being.

The other attempt was the craft guilds. The schools of alchemy largely failed whilst the schools of craft produced notable and striking success. Throughout Europe the craft guilds established schools and training centers to which young people were admitted as apprentices. After a number of years of training, including menial tasks necessary to the craft, they ascended to the second degree of fellow, mate, or journeyman. To this craft training was linked the fascinating wisdom that the young person in training had to leave home, town and country. After achieving a certain amount of learning the fellow or mate had to set out on a long journey spanning a number of years and covering a considerable area of Europe. This was done because the type of training given by a craft guild would unavoidably bind and limit a craftsman to a certain place in society. Before that sacrifice could be made, it was necessary for the learning craftsman to have time to wander and encounter as much of the world as possible. The third degree of training was that of master, the one who achieved the perfect incarnation of the plan into a given material.

Try to hold onto the few basic ideas, which we have encountered. First, craft incarnates, through the organ of the human hand, a pre-existing form into earthly material. One can sense here a fundamental Christian principle: Christ in his youth, as the Man Jesus, can be imagined as the Craftsman. In all cultures it is the image in which he is seen, and Craft is the exercise that implants, through the hand, spirit into matter. We may feel that this has something to do with morality in the highest sense. The problem which arises in our time is that we have not found a new way to do what the crafts from the Middle Ages to the beginning of this century did for the moral existence of the human being. The development that started with the Industrial Revolution caused the physical economic justification of craft to disappear. What has been done as a purely spiritual exercise and at the same time satisfied man's basic material need, was pushed away through the developments at the end of the last century. Modern production methods have made craft impossible and have not as yet allowed for the development of another form in which to realize the spiritual and moral aspect of craft.

Britain and other countries are now looked upon as being lazy and incapable of competing in the labor force. Large groups of men frequently come out in protest knowing that this will cause serious hardship to their country. The reason is not simply the desire for increased monetary return for their labor. They earn more each year but, with the rising cost of living, their earnings remain more or less the same. But this is not the issue. The issue is that, though they may have a bit more to eat and wear and have cars, they must also find their moral dignity—and they cannot find it. They hope to find it by setting off one guild trade union against another. They try to introduce differentials, to work slowly and deliberately, because that instills the memory of craftwork in them. Craftwork is basically a differentiated, organized way of incarnating spirit into matter. This happens individually in the craftsman when he relates his work to his hands. He may not know it, but it happens and cannot be done in a hurry. When man is robbed of it he senses his deprivation and degradation. He needs what only the craft can do—creation of moral substance.

At this point I would like to describe the skeletal nature of the human hand. We can hold our palms so that it looks upward, or so that the palm looks downwards—supination or pronation. We can do this because between the upper arm and hand there are two bones, the radius and ulna. When the two bones are parallel our hand looks upwards, when crossed, downwards. The foot is similarly built but we can no longer turn the foot; it is permanently turned down onto the earth.

In the description in the Gospels of Good Friday, the Roman soldiers broke the bones of the two who were crucified on either side of the Christ, but they did not break His bones. It was said in the Scriptures: "His bones shall not be broken." This does not refer only to the external but to the archetypal fact that our feet were unbroken before we descended to earth. We have retained only in our hands the freedom of turning upwards to the world of our origin. Craft uses this organ to descend in freedom into the bondage of earthly matter, thus expressing the divine essence of the human being.

II

Let us face the very difficult issue of morality so that we can see its connection to craft. When we consider the beginning of morality, how it emerged out of primeval time and displayed itself in history, it is quite obvious that the issue of morality arises with that of good and evil. The description in Genesis is magnificent—the birth of Good and Evil in the consciousness of Man when, living in Paradise under the direct guidance of divinity, he transgressed the original command and ate of the forbidden fruit of knowledge. This is the moment when his eyes were opened and he knew Good and Evil. Morality has throughout history been variously linked, and especially in our time, to the question of sex. However, it is written that when Adam ate of the Tree of Knowledge his eyes were opened, the world appeared and he knew that he too could be seen by the light. Thus the problem of Good and Evil is presented as the problem of knowledge. But is the problem of morality one of knowledge? I do not think that it is. I think that morality is the opposite of knowledge.

In modern times we have learned to highly value pure intelligence. We educate our children to the greatest possible intellectual independence. They learn to look up all answers in textbooks so that they can become as self-reliant as possible. They become ever more clever, and when they leave school they understand that they are now meant to be successful. They set out to find out how they can best provide money, they read papers, statistics, and they inform themselves. Obviously morality does not flow from that source. I describe this to show that it is not so simple to interpret the primeval story of eating the apple of knowledge as morality. It is a most puzzling and difficult problem.

Various widely divergent moral codes exist. Probably all of us and the majority of the population of the Western world would agree that highjacking trucks filled with electronic media is not moral. Among Eskimo tribes they have the practice of allowing their elderly to leave their camps to go into the wilderness to be eaten by wild animals; the old people accept this as their duty. In certain African tribes when a child is born and before it is fed, it is shown to the father; if he considers it to be imperfect it is destroyed. For us these codes of behavior are shocking.

Another thing that seems to have been universal up to the time of Christ, and is still held as a high moral code by some small groups of modern man, is the principle of vengeance. The value of a man was measured by the degree of persistence in avenging any offense done to his family. A man who would take an offense unrevenged would become an outcast. It is still the case in some parts of Sicily, so intensely valued as a moral code that imprisonment for life as a result of an act of revenge is accepted. Interestingly, to many revenge is not only not a very important issue, but the more modern we are, the less we possess the power of revenge. Those who still maintain a strong heritage from the past have slightly greater capacity for revenge, but a truly modern person forgets an offense. [An exception is the modern Moslem and

Israeli cultures that still take revenge very seriously.] This is a mysterious fact. Moral values seem to arise from a far greater depth than our ideas.

Moral codes may vary tremendously in the course of time—and equally in different cultures and societies. They vary even within the same society, in different levels and different age groups.

Cultured Asian people are trained to say that which the other wishes to hear. The factual truth would be regarded as impolite. They feel morally obliged to tell lies for reasons of politeness and do so every day.

We have made the problem still more confused. I should like briefly to describe something that Rudolf Steiner said about morality in a lecture course to teachers of the first Waldorf school. He spoke then not about morality but about will: the problem of morality is actually a problem of the will and not of the thinking. Steiner said that there are three aspects in the forces of the human soul: thinking, feeling, and willing. While thinking is the soul's ability to relate images in the soul in an ordered way, will is the source of action but is completely hidden from consciousness. If I lift a glass of water, it is an action of my body. The glass of water can be in my consciousness and I can have the intention of lifting it—but nothing happens, i.e., there is a difference between intention and action. And this difference we call will. If I will to lift the glass, I can lift it, but if I only think about it I may not lift it. Obviously there is a world of difference in the will and yet it is a world that does not appear in my consciousness. This is an essential aspect of morality—we are apparently involved fundamentally in a realm which, to begin with, is not accessible to our consciousness. Our will is completely asleep and is yet the most real and consequential way in which we are put into this world.

Steiner describes something very interesting about the polarity of thinking and willing: Our feeling is interplay between the two. Our feeling is will that has not yet stepped into the reality of action; if intensified towards reality it becomes will. Further, our feeling is a confluence in which a certain slight will tendency meets the image tendency in our thinking so that our soul experiences, though not consciously as a thought, but in a kind of dream consciousness. Steiner then makes the following statement: Our existence on earth is determined from two sides. The physical body is prepared from heredity in order that something of a purely spiritual nature can manifest. This is very much the picture of craft! There must be a plan. A table must exist in concept, an ideal. Once tables exist the craftsman can, with the help of suitable materials and tools, bring about the materialization of the idea of a table. Equally, if the individuality of man did not spiritually exist, we could not incarnate as infants and develop as persons on earth.

Our type of thinking, feeling, and willing is not part of the eternal idea of the human being but is part of incarnated human being on earth. Steiner says that we enter from a purely spiritual existence through birth and begin to work in our physical hereditary body. In a given environment we work out our destiny on earth and unfold the three soul forces. We have been thrust out of a previous existence and the door shut. Hardly any man on earth has any memory of what he was before he was born (though a few poets have had faint glimpses of this pre-birth existence). It belongs to our human existence on earth that the door is shut: we are really thrown out. The force that closes the door when we are born is the source of the force within us, which gradually develops in us the power of a mirror.

Do we know why we see ourselves in a mirror? What makes a mirror show us ourselves? Why do not other substances reflect? It must be a mirror, a polished surface. As long as substance or a piece of material receives the light that falls upon it, it will not mirror. But once it becomes shut off from the light, everything is thrown back and the approaching light is straight away reflected. This is the nature of a mirror: this is the nature of thinking. It is a mistake when someone takes the grimace in the mirror as a threat and hits back. Many wars have arisen not because we want to hurt one another but because we are frightened that the other may hurt us. This is a most typical situation in the destiny of humankind: that he does not know himself, that he does not know that the fear in the other is the mirror picture of himself. This is the force of thinking, the mirror force arises because when we were born we left and were shut out from the other world. We bear that force with us and the further away from the other world we grow, the stronger the mirroring force.

But we go towards another gate, that of death. In reality with our first breath we go towards death. That is will. If we think that to be born is not to die we delude ourselves—but the harmony, which arises between the two is our feeling.

Why have I told you all this? It is basic but has little to do with morality. Steiner says the following: The will which leads us back to our own existence is the only thing in us which is individual. Thinking is universal, we share our thinking with all human beings. If we read today Plato or Aristotle we can ask whether we have really developed. Comparing any philosopher of the past with those of the present we have to admit that they knew it all. There is no real progress in thinking. But read Plato and you will see that in his time there were slaves. Divine authority ordained this. Read Paul, that most modern of men, and see that he advises slaves to do what their masters tell them and to be grateful because they are his masters. How we would revolt against such feelings. Our feelings and values are totally different. We have made fantastic strides feelingwise. Why? Because this is truly individual: it leads always to the future. We do not intrinsically hold moral codes in common with all mankind. We hold such codes in common with groups of men because they flow from the will and begin to dawn in our feeling man. How is it with the source of morality that we suspect belongs here? Morality is mine: that makes it morality. It is not that I conform to a social code: this I may do but I know that it is not my morality. My morality is that little wellspring, utterly individual, that I do it. The agreed norm is not morality but that at a special moment I do this—that is morality.

Steiner says the following: Will works in everything that is alive—not only in the human being but in everything that is divine and incarnated. It works in the individual through his fourfold nature: through his physical organization; into his living, etheric organization, into his emotional, astral organization as well as into human ego nature.

What does the will do in the physical body? It creates instinct. The fact that beavers can fell trees so that they fall to form a dam, or that bees collect pollen from far distant plants, produce, and deposit the wax in such a way that a honeycomb—one of the most highly differentiated, mechanical structures—arises, this is instinct. Will working in the physical. Will working in the life processes creates drive, forces that govern modern life, govern nutrition, the excreting of substances, procreation. Will working in the emotional creates desires, longings, passions. Will working in our essentially ego nature creates something that, though it is probably the most important aspect of human existence, is hardly known as a word—motivation.

In our schools we have increasing numbers of children who are very intelligent—often moreso than their teachers—yet they are completely incapable of living harmoniously with other people and fitting into society. They may be able to do very intricate things but they perhaps cannot eat at a table with other people. Sometimes one says that they are emotionally disturbed children but sometimes they are completely undisturbed and undisturbable, because if motivation rolls too far no feeling arises. They are not disturbed in their feeling, they are impartial.

There are many things that one is capable of doing but would not do because one has a harmoniously integrated motivation, one is in one world with everybody else. We have a highly integrated, well-fitting common world out of our organized, differentiated motivation. Imagine that we were a group of twenty lions, five cows, three seagulls, and so forth. It is not the lack of intelligence in the seagull that would cause a problem but a completely different motivation. We are capable of living together as human beings only because there is an all-pervading motivation among us. Most crimes of today are a breakdown in motivation. They can be brilliantly engineered and efforts are made not to injure anyone. What they want to do obviously must be done in the best way possible.

Not only does the will in the human create motivation, it does something else. Steiner says that though will brings about motivation, there is by necessity a slight discrepancy between the idea and physical execution. For example, I think a point and the point I think is mathematical; it has no size. Whether I make such a point on the blackboard or with the sharpest of pencils, it is unavoidably a blotch. It lies in the nature of things. Anything that is physically present only approaches approximate perfection. You cannot think a wrong 90° triangle. And that lies equally in the nature of the spiritual. Therefore, whatever we bring about through motivation practically can never express the idea. That is the link with craft. When we make something with our hands we are responsible for it. If I sow corn it is not my work but divine enactment, which makes it grow. If I teach a child and the child learns have I brought this about? Learning is an activity of the child and not of the teacher.

Steiner said that because of the relationship between the physical and spiritual, when we have done something with our hands craftwise, there usually remains an unsatisfied element of wish: I could have done better. This is the seed for incarnation into consciousness of the next higher divine principle of the human being, beyond his ego.

We are distinguished from animals because we know our own ego. Animals have much more majestic spiritual beings behind them, the wisdom of all cattle not only domesticated, is far greater than the wisdom of individual man. But the individual cow has not got it and is only part of it. She is directed by a great spiritual power.

We have a glimpse of our spiritual nature, the lowest bit of the totality of man's spirit. The totality of man's spirit exists but it is God. In the end this divinity wants to live completely in the human being as it once lived in Jesus. This is the meaning of human existence. It is slow, there is time, and we must always do something about it to bring into incarnation or manifestation the divinity.

Nobody can deny that if we look at the human being and the world from the viewpoint of natural science, there is nothing divine in the human being. On the contrary, the human being appears as one of the animals with peculiar habits. He is only part of a tremendous universe. We are endowed with another way of looking at all this, but it is not fashionable because the human being is convinced that he should be born but not die. This is at the root of many of our problems. Though we can survive if born prematurely noone wishes to be so born. Equally, no one wishes to die prematurely. But because he does not wish a premature birth, it does not mean he does not wish to be born. But it is a largely accepted fact that not only do we not wish for premature death, but feeling-wise we do not wish to die at all. This is a fallacy and not human.

When the will works in the ego bringing about motivation, there remains the wish to do something better. Steiner speaks of two further steps: the resolution that can arise and the decision that can follow. This lived in the Middle Ages in the craftwork. It is the morality-creating power of craft, something only conceptually known embodied by the human hand into matter and never absolutely perfect. This is par excellence the fine wish to do better.

This and nothing else is morality. Although it works out feeling-wise into a variety of moral codes, morality is the human being's willingness to bring to greater realization his/her divine nature. This is motivation and we have to strive for it in our time not in physical work with our hands but in the encounter of one human being and another. When I greet someone in the morning there must arise in my soul the wish that I should be able to do that better—even only just that greeting, as, if we are truly honest, we know that we have in fact shied from giving a true greeting. We have become so sensitive and so much on the threshold of new motivation that we feel in every meeting with another person the wish to do better. If we will learn to listen to that wish in our soul, we shall have provided a foothold for further development of morality.

Forces Leading to Health and Illness in Education

by

Rudolf Steiner

translated by René Querido

By permeating our knowledge with anthroposophy, it is possible to unfold a vital life of soul. We need this vital soul life if we wish to have the strength for our teaching and education. I would like to speak to you now about something that is pre-eminently a goal to strive for in education, namely, that through a particular orientation in educational activity, inner forces can be gathered in order to fire the heart in an educational sense.

Today I wish to speak to the following question: With what forces are we really working when we work educationally? Actually, this question cannot be answered in any definite sense by the culture of today. We can say, of course, that the outer life, within which human beings stand, making it possible for them to earn a living, requires them to have capacities that they cannot have yet as children. We must impart such capacities to them. The behavior proper for adults is also, perhaps, something that the child cannot acquire by himself; it must be imparted to him through education. But the answer to the question of why do we actually educate remains something rather superficial in modern culture, because the adult today does not really see anything of great value in what he became through the teaching and education he received. He does not look back with any particularly deep gratitude to what he has become through his education. Ask yourself in your own heart whether this gratitude is always alive in you. In individual cases, of course, it may be present on reflection, but on the whole we do not think with deep gratitude about our own education, because the human soul does not have a full realization of what education actually means, nor which forces in human nature are quickened by it. That is why it is so difficult nowadays to arouse in people enthusiasm for education. All our methods, all our ingenious, formed, outer methods of education, are of little value in this respect. Answers to the question how can this or that be achieved are of little use.

What is of the greatest importance, however, is for a person to have enthusiasm in his work and, if he is to be a true teacher, to be able to develop this enthusiasm to the full. This enthusiasm is infectious, and it alone can work miracles in education. The child eagerly responds to enthusiasm, and, when there is no response on his part, it usually indicates a lack of this enthusiasm in the teacher. As a kind of obvious secret, let me say that although a great deal has been said about enthusiasm here, when I go through the classes in the school I see a kind of depression, a kind of heaviness in the teachers.

The lessons are often conducted with certain heaviness. This heaviness must be eliminated. Actually, it may also express itself in artificial enthusiasm. Artificial enthusiasm can achieve nothing at all. The only enthusiasm capable of achieving anything is that kindled by our own living interest in the subjects with which we must deal in the classroom.

Now, it is essential for you to realize that as teachers we need to develop a consciousness of our own. It is necessary for us to work at cultivating this consciousness. This work to develop our own consciousness is certainly made infinitely more difficult by the fact that in the higher grades we must take into account the impossible demands made upon our children from outside in preparation for graduation. This lies like a leaden burden upon the teaching in the higher grades. Nevertheless, it is essential not to lose sight of our own goal, and therefore we must work to develop this consciousness, the Waldorf teacher's consciousness, if I may so express it. This is only possible, however, when in the field of education we come to an actual experience of the spiritual. Such an experience of the spiritual is difficult to attain for modern humanity, and this fact must be faced and understood. We must realize that we really need something quite specific, something that is hardly present anywhere else in the world, if we are to be capable of mastering the task of the Waldorf school. In all humility, without any trace of pride or arrogance, we must become conscious of this, but conscious of it inwardly, deep in our hearts, not merely by talking about it; within our hearts we must be able to become conscious of it. This is possible, however, only if we have a clear understanding of what humanity has lost in this respect, has lost just in the last three or four centuries. It is this that we must find again.

What has been lost is the realization that when the human being enters the world out of his pre-earthly existence, he is, compared with the actual forces of the being of man, a being who needs to be healed. This bond of education with the healing of man has been lost from sight. During a certain period of the Middle Ages, certainly, it was believed that the human being, as man on earth, was ill and that his health had to be restored; that the human being as he was on the earth actually stood below his proper level and that something real had to be done in order to make man truly man. This is often understood merely in a formal sense. It is said that the human being must evolve, must be brought to a higher level, but this is meant abstractly, not concretely. It will be interpreted concretely only when the activity of education is actually brought into connection with the activity of healing. In healing a sick person, one knows that something has actually been achieved: if the sick person has been made healthy, he has been raised to a higher level, to the level of the normal human being. In ancient times those who knew the world mysteries regarded birth as synonymous with illness, because, in fact, when the human being is born he falls in a certain sense below his proper level and is not the being he was in pre-earthly existence. In comparison with the higher human nature, it is really something abnormal for the human being to bear within him constituents of his body, to have to bear certain heaviness. It would not be considered particularly intelligent today to say that, in comparison with the higher nature of man, it is of the nature of illness to have to struggle continually until death with the physical forces of the body. Without such radical conceptions, however, we cannot approach the reality of what education means. Education must have something of the process of healing. In order to make this clear, let me offer the following.

The human being really lives within four complexes of forces. In one he is active when he walks, moves his legs with a pendulum swing, or when he uses his legs in order to dance or make other movements. This movement, taking place in the outer, physical world of space, can also be pictured as bringing about changes of location in space. Similarly, other possibilities of human movement, of the arms, hands, head, eye muscles, and so forth, can be designated as changes in location of an ordinary inanimate body, that is to say, if we leave out of account the inner activity of the human being. This is one complex of forces within which the human being lives and is active.

The second is unfolded when man begins to work upon the physical substances that he absorbs into himself; in the widest sense this includes everything that belongs to the activity of nourishment. Whereas the limbs of man are the mediators of what man has in common with beings that change their physical location, there is another activity that man needs in order to continue the activity connected with the outer substances that man absorbs as nourishment. If you put a piece of sugar into your mouth, it dissolves. This is a continuation of what sugar is in the outer world. Sugar is hard and white. You dissolve it, and it becomes liquid, viscous, and then undergoes further changes. The chemist speaks of chemical changes, but that is not relevant here. The sugar continually changes. It is worked upon and absorbed into the whole organism. There you have a second kind of activity. This continues right into the rhythmic system, and then the rhythmic system takes over the activity of the digestive system. What happens in this second kind of activity of man, however, is very different from the human activity of moving the limbs or of moving the whole human body in the outer world. The activity of nourishment is quite different from the activity exercised when we move outwardly or, let us say, lift a weight. This activity of nourishment cannot proceed at all without the intervention, at every point of this activity, of the astral nature of the human being. The astral nature of the human being must permeate each individual part of this activity, of nourishment. In the activity that I have described as the activity of walking, grasping, and so on, we are dealing essentially with the same forces man makes use of that we can also verify physically. What really happens in these movements is that the etheric organism is set in motion and through its mediation arises a leverage movement that we can see in an act of grasping or walking. If we focus on the activity of walking or grasping, we need only consider that which we have in the physical world as it is inserted within the working of the etheric; then we have what happens in man. We never have this, however, if we consider the activity of nourishment. This can arise only if the astral body takes hold of processes that otherwise we have in the test tube. There astral forces above all must be at work, and a fact that is considered nary at all is that in this process physical forces no longer play a part. This is exceedingly interesting, because it is generally believed that in nourishment, for example, physical forces are at work. As soon as the human being no longer exists in relation to the outer world, the physical forces cease to have their *raison d'etre*; they are no longer active, no longer have any effect. In the activity of nourishment, the physical substances are worked upon by the astral and etheric. The physical effect of a piece of sulfur or salt outside the body has no significance within the body. Only the astral nature of a substance is seized or taken hold of by the astral, and then the etheric-astral is the really active factor in nourishment.

Going further, we come to the activities taking place in the rhythmic nature of man, in the blood rhythm, in the breathing rhythm. In their inner constitution these activities are similar to the forces at work in the system of nourishment. They are the result of cooperation between the etheric and the astral, but in the activity of digestion the astral is in a certain respect weaker than the etheric, and in the rhythmic activity the astral becomes stronger than the etheric. In the rhythmic system the etheric withdraws more into the background (though actually only the etheric that is *within* the human being). The etheric outside the human being begins to take part again in the activity that is exercised in the rhythmic system of man, so that actually with the activity of breathing one has the force of man's inner etheric body, the force of the outer ether of the world, and the astral activity of man.

Now, picture to yourselves what is really going on when the human being breathes. The physical activity of carbon, oxygen, and so forth, is completely suppressed, but the combined working of the etheric outside, the etheric within, and the astral is a most important factor. This plays a great part. These are the forces, however, that we must know in any substance if we wish to speak of the healing effect of that substance. We cannot discover the extent to which a substance is a remedy if we do not know how that substance, when introduced into the body, is laid hold of by these three systems of forces. The whole of therapy depends upon knowledge of these three forces in connection with the substances used. Knowledge of the healing influence in the outer and inner etheric and in the astral is what constitutes therapy in the real sense. What does it mean when antimony, for example, is used as a remedy? It simply means that some form of antimony is introduced into the body; it is laid hold of in a certain way by the inner etheric forces, by the outer etheric forces that enter by way of the breathing, and by the astral forces in the human being. We realize the extent to which antimony is a remedy when we understand the effect of these three systems of forces on a substance within the human organism.[3]

In ascending to the rhythmic activity, therefore, we come to recognize a much more delicate process than exists, for example, in the activity of nourishment. It is essentially this rhythmic activity that must be considered if we wish to recognize the healing effects. Unless we know how a particular substance affects the rhythm of breathing or the blood circulation, we cannot understand the nature of this substance as a remedy.

Now the strange thing is this. Whereas the doctor brings into operation the therapeutic forces in the unconscious, in the rhythmic system of the blood circulation or the breathing, as teachers we must bring the next higher stage into operation: that which is connected with the activity in the nerves, in the senses. This is the next metamorphosis of the remedy. What we do as teachers is really to work in such a way on the physical human being that the substances that are taken up are subjected to the etheric activity and to the outer physical activity—namely, to perception, whenever something is perceived—and to the inner physical activity, that is to say, to the inner changes of location brought about mechanically through the human being's moving himself. Whereas in the remedy are contained the outer and inner etheric and the astral, in education are contained outer physical forces (as in gymnastics) and inner physical forces. When the human being bows his head, a change takes place in his entire dynamic system; the center of gravity shifts a little, and so forth. In the workings of light upon the eye we recognize outer physical forces in their greatest delicacy and refinement. Moreover, outer physical forces are operating when pressure is made on an organ of touch. We therefore have etheric activity, outer physical forces, and inner physical forces, that is to say, physical changes in the nervous system, destruction in the nervous system. These are true physical processes that are actually present only in the nervous system of the human being. It is with these three systems that we are essentially dealing as a teacher with the child. This is the higher metamorphosis of what is done in healing.

What kinds of activity are present in the human being? There are the movements of walking, grasping, the movement of the limbs, outer changes of location, the activity in the process of nourishment, the rhythmic activity—which is through and through a healing activity—and the perceiving activity if we regard it from outside. Regarded from within, educational activity is entirely a perceiving activity.

This will now give you deeper insight into the nature of the human being. You will be able to say to yourselves that, since factors are active in the rhythmic system that are healing factors, there is a doctor continually present in the human being. In fact, the whole rhythmic system is a doctor. The function of a doctor is to heal something, however, and if healing is needed there must be illness. If that is so, walking, grasping, digesting must be continual processes of illness, and breathing and blood circulation a continual healing. This is indeed the case. In modern science, however, where discrimination is lacking, it is not realized that the human being is continually becoming ill. Eating and drinking, especially, are processes that continually create illness. We cannot avoid continually injuring our health through eating and drinking. Eating and drinking to excess merely injure us more seriously, but we are always injuring ourselves to a slight degree. The rhythmic system, however, is continually healing this illness. Human life on the earth is a continual process of becoming ill and healing. This process of becoming ill brings about a genuinely physical illness. What the human being does in intercourse with the outer world, the consequences of walking, grasping, and the like, is a more intense but less noticeable process of becoming ill. We must counter it through a higher process of healing, through a process of education, which is a metamorphosis of the healing process.

The forces inherent in education are metamorphoses of therapeutic forces: they are therapeutic forces transformed. The goal of all our educational thinking must be to transform this thinking so as to rise fruitfully from the level of physical thinking to spiritual thinking. In physical thinking we have two categories which, in our academic age, give rise to a vacuous enthusiasm that has such a terrible influence. We have only two concepts: right-wrong, true-false. To discover whether something is "true" or "false" is the highest ideal of those whose entire lives are given up to the world of academia. In the concepts "true" and "false," however, there is so little reality. They are something formal, established by mere logic, which actually does nothing but combine and separate. The concepts of "true" and "false" are dreadfully barren, prosaic, and formal. The moment we rise to the truths of the spiritual world we can no longer speak of "true" and "false," for in the spiritual world that would be as nonsensical as saying that to drink such and such a quantity of wine every day is "false." The expression "false" here is out of place. One says something real regarding this only by saying that such a thing gives rise to illness. "Correct" and "incorrect" are outer, formal concepts, even regarding the physical. Pertaining to the spiritual world, the concepts of "true" and "false" should be discarded altogether. As soon as we reach the spiritual world we must substitute "healthy" and "ill" for "true" and "false." If someone said about a lecture, such as the one I gave here yesterday evening, that is "right," it would mean nothing at all. In the physical world things can be "right"; in the spiritual world nothing is "wrong" or "right." There, things are reality. After all, is a hunchback "true" or "false"? In such a case we cannot speak of right or wrong. A drawing may be false or correct, but not a plant; a plant however, can be healthy or diseased. In the spiritual world things are either healthy or ill, fruitful or unfruitful. In what one does there must be reality. If someone considers that a lecture such as I gave yesterday is healthy or health-bringing, that is to the point. If he simply considers it "right," he merely shows that he cannot rise to the level where reality lies. It is a question of health or illness when we are dealing with spiritual truths, and it is precisely this that we must learn in connection with education. We must learn to regard things in their educational application as either healthy or unhealthy, as healing or injurious to health. This is of particular significance if one wishes to engender a true consciousness of oneself as a teacher. It may be said that engendering this consciousness begins with passing from the "true" and "false" of logic, to the reality of "healthy" or "unhealthy." Then we come quite close to understanding the principle of healing. This can be developed in concrete detail, but we must also let ourselves be stimulated by a comprehensive knowledge of the human being, a knowledge of the human being in relation to the world around him.

In describing the breathing process, for example, according to modern science, no particular weight is laid on the essential factor, on the actual human factor. It is said that the air consists of oxygen and nitrogen, leaving aside for the moment the other constituents. The human being inhales oxygen along with a certain amount of nitrogen. He then exhales oxygen combined with carbon, and also nitrogen. The percentages are measured, and it is believed that the essentials of the process have been described. Little account is taken, however, of the essentially human factor. This begins to dawn upon us when we consider the following. There is a definite percentage of nitrogen in the air that is good for breathing, and also a definite percentage of oxygen. Suppose a man comes to a region where the air is poor in nitrogen, containing less than the normal percentage. If the person breathes in this nitrogen-poor air, this air gradually becomes richer in nitrogen through his breathing. He exhales from his body nitrogen that he would not otherwise exhale in order to augment the nitrogen content of the air in his environment. I do not know whether any account is taken of this in physiology today. I have often pointed out that the human being living in air that is poor in nitrogen corrects this lack; he prefers to take nitrogen from his own organic substances, depriving them of it in order to augment the nitrogen content of the outside air. He does the same with respect to the normal content of oxygen in the air. The human being is so intimately related to his environment that the moment the environment is not as it ought to be, he corrects it, improves upon it. We may say then that the human being is constituted in such a way that he needs nitrogen and oxygen not only for himself; it is even more necessary for him to have nitrogen and oxygen in certain percentages in his environment than within his own organism. The environment of a human being is more important for his subconscious forces than the make-up of his own body. The incredibly interesting fact is that through his instincts the human being has a far greater interest in his environment than in the make-up of his own body. This is something that can be proved by experiment, provided the experiments are arranged intelligently. It is only a question of arranging experiments in this realm. If our research institutes would only tackle such problems, what a vast amount there would be for them to do! The problems are there and are of tremendous importance. They are terribly important for education, too, for it is only now that we can ask why the human being needs an environment containing a particular amount of nitrogen and a particular amount of oxygen. We know that in the inner activity of nourishment or general growth, all kinds of combinations of substances are formed in the human being, revealing themselves in a particular way when man becomes a corpse. It is only in this dead form, however, that these things are investigated by science today.

Now the strange thing is that in the sphere of the human being that encompasses part of the rhythmic activity and part of the metabolic-limb activity, there is a tendency for an activity to unfold between carbon and nitrogen. In the sphere that extends from the rhythmic upward to the nerve-sense activity, there is a tendency to unfold an activity between carbon and oxygen. It is truly interesting, if one observes with a soul constitution not worn out by dry scholarship, to take a look at sparkling soda water, where the carbon dioxide appears in the liquid as the result of the interplay of carbon and oxygen. If one observes these bubbles, one has directly and imaginatively a view of what goes on in the course of the rhythmic breathing activity from the lung system toward the head. The bubbling effervescence in sparkling water is a picture of what, in a fine and delicate way, plays upward toward the human head. Looking at a spring of sparkling water, we can say that this activity of the rising carbon dioxide is really similar, only in a coarser form, to a continual, inward activity within the human being that rises from the lungs to the head. In the head, something must continually be stimulated by a delicate, intimate sparkling-water activity; otherwise, the human being becomes stupid or dull. If we neglect to bring this effervescence of sparkling water to the head of a human being, then the carbon within him suddenly shows an inclination for hydrogen instead of oxygen. This rises up to the brain and produces "marsh gas," such as is found in subterranean vaults, and then the human being becomes dull, drowsy, and musty.

To begin with, these things confront us as inner—one would like to say—physical activities, but they are not really physical, for the production of marsh gas or carbon dioxide becomes in this case an inner spiritual activity. We are not being led into materialism here but into the delicate weaving of the spiritual in matter.

Now if, in teaching languages, for example, we make the child learn too much vocabulary, if we make him memorize through an unconscious mechanization, this process can lead to the development of marsh gas in the head. If we bring as many living pictures as possible to the child, the effect is such that the breathing system lets the carbon dioxide effervesce toward the head. We therefore play a part, in fact, in something that makes for either health or illness. This shows us how as teachers we must demand a higher metamorphosis of the forces of healing. To be able to perceive these hidden relationships in the human organism kindles enthusiasm in the highest degree. We realize for the first time that the head is a remarkable vault that can be filled with either marsh gas or carbon dioxide. We feel we are standing before the deeper wellsprings of existence.

In the next lecture we shall study another activity, with which this activity must be brought into balance. This can happen, however, only when there is on the one hand the right kind of teaching in the musical sphere and, on the other, the right kind of teaching in lessons that are based upon outer perception and not upon the musical sphere. Thus, our teaching takes shape, and our interest is aroused in the human being before us. To this something else must be added: the feeling of responsibility. The consciousness of a Waldorf teacher should be imbued with the realization that makes him say in all humility: People are let loose into the educational world today as if the totally blind were sent out to paint in color. Few know what is really taking place in education. It is no wonder that a blind man has no particular enthusiasm for painting in color; no wonder there is no real enthusiasm for education in the world! The moment we enter into education in the way described, however, the whole art of our education will provide the stimulus for this enthusiasm, and we shall feel that we are in touch with the wellsprings of the world, and find the true feeling of responsibility. We will realize that we can bring about either health or illness. This enthusiasm on the one hand and a feeling of responsibility on the other—both must arise in us.

Additional Lectures from Rudolf Steiner on Moral Education

Title	Book
"Pedagogy and Art"	GA 36 Lecture notes
"Pedagogy and Morality"	GA 36 Lecture notes
	GA 304a Stuttgart, March 26, 1923
	GA 304a The Hague November 19, 1923
	GA 305 Lecture Oxford Course August 24, 1922
	GA 218 Lecture London November 19, 1922
"The Education of Children from the Perspective of Spiritual Science"	GA 34 Lecture Article in "Lucifer Gnosis," 1907
"Striving People of Our Times"	GA 176 Lecture "Truths of Humanity's Development" Berlin, July 3, 1917
"Paths of Spriritual Knowledge and the Renewal of Artistic Morality"	Dornach February 2, 1915 GA 079
"The Educational Practice"	GA 306
"Social Understanding from Spiritual Science"	GA 191 November 14, 1919

Transformative Education and the Right to an Inviolate Childhood

by

Christopher Clouder

Dostoyevsky's earliest memory comes from when he was three years old. He was brought into a room by his governess and asked, in the presence of some guests, to say his evening prayers. Kneeling before the icon he began "Dear Mother God, all my hope is in Thee—give me shelter under Thy wing." This prayer he never forgot. He taught it to his own children and repeated it throughout his life.[1]

This event, from the early decade of the last century, is far removed from the experience of most children of today. A deep-seated attitude of reverence, developed and nurtured in the very early years, is for nearly all the world's children a thing of the past. The tensions and turbulence of our times leave little space for such attitudes to be fostered. Hence the growing debate about values and spirituality in education and the bringing up of children that has become an important aspect of current concerns. Louis MacNeice's poem "Prayer before Birth" is more indicative of our times.

I am not yet born; console me.
I fear that the human race may with tall walls wall me,
    with strong drugs dope me, with wise lies lure me,
        on black racks rack me, in blood-baths roll me.

I am not yet born; forgive me.
For the sins that in me the world shall commit, my words
    when they speak me, my thoughts when they think me,
        my treason engendered by traitors beyond me,
            my life when they murder by means of my
                hands, my death when they live me.

I am not yet born; 0 fill me
With strength against those who would freeze my
    humanity, would dragoon me into a lethal automaton,
        would make me a cog in a machine, a thing with
            one face, a thing, and against all those
                who would dissipate my entirety, would
                    blow me like thistledown hither and

> thither or hither and thither
> like water held in the
> hands would spill me.²

When we speak of the right to an inviolate childhood it becomes a truism. No right-thinking adult is against it, yet many children do face a world that contains threats to their healthy and happy development, as outlined in this poem. And MacNeice's conclusion is a stark one:

Let them not make me a stone and let them not spill me.
Otherwise kill me.

This is the antithesis of the hope and joy that each child brings into life at birth. Rembrandt's paintings of Christ's birth in a stable at Bethlehem, where the light streaming from the child shines into the surrounding darkness and embraces even the most humble of creatures in the dismal areas of the structure, are a depiction of a universal truth. A newborn baby brings light and love with it that can illuminate all the recesses of the human heart. As adults we participate in an intuitive wonder that draws us towards the baby:

It is of extraordinary significance that we, in our descent into earthly life, draw together forces from the universal ether, and thus take with us, in our ether body, a kind of image of the cosmos. If one could extract the human ether body at the moment when the human being is uniting himself with the physical body, we should have a sphere which is far more beautiful than any formed by mechanical means—a sphere containing stars, zodiac, sun and moon.³

A child is born into a social context. "And she brought forth her first born son, and wrapped him in swaddling clothes and laid him in a manger." The binding of an infant to prevent movement, as though still enwrapped and protected by the womb, is still practiced in some cultures. In others it is seen as detrimental to a child's need to exercise its limbs and move freely, thereby stimulating the senses. Our social and cultural differences manifest themselves from the first breath onwards and are part of the child's learning process in becoming a social being. Rudolf Steiner tells us that in earlier cultures children were born with innate social capacities but in our times these abilities have to be learned. This underlines our need to understand—and to work with greater insight—the evolution of consciousness and cultures if we are to serve the needs of young children in a healthy and desirable manner.

Firstly, a child should be welcomed. How that welcome is expressed can vary according to the times and the social fabric around the child. A report from the Swedish Aid Commission touches on elements that confront us as citizens of the affluent minority world.

Basic to a good society is that children are welcome, are given a good environment during childhood and are the concern of the whole society. Children have a right to secure living conditions that enhance their development. Preschool has an important function in children's lives. It offers a comprehensive program and is the source of stimulation in the children's development. It gives them a chance to meet other children and adults and to be part of an experience of fellowship and friendship. It is a complement to the upbringing a child gets at home.[4]

For many children, Ellen Key's concept of the "Century of Childhood" has brought countless benefits, though it is salutary to remember that children in the majority world have not yet been enabled to share these welcome changes to the same extent. At the beginning of the century, the infant mortality rate for most European countries was within the range of 100 to 250 deaths per 1000 live births. By the 1950s this had fallen to between 25 and 50, by 1995 only three European countries had rates of above 20, and only one, Albania, above 30. In Western European countries it is now well below 10.[5] We have moved from a time when the death of a baby was a tragic—but expected—family event, one which parents were rarely able to avoid, to a time when we can assume that our children will reach adulthood. This is completely new in the history of childhood and is of great significance to our attitude to parenting. There are fewer siblings in a family and children are not so greatly separated by age. They grow up differently.

Ellen Key, the Swedish educational reformer and feminist, published her influential book *The Century of the Child* in 1900:

> The next century will be the century of the child just as much as the last century has been the woman's century. When the child gets his rights, morality will be perfect. The role of a woman was to devote herself to the care of children, hygiene and sick nursing. Kindergartens and crèches were only second best, and schools should strive to make themselves redundant. Success in child rearing lay in becoming *as a child oneself*. The simplicity of the child's character will be kept as adults. So the old social order will renew itself.[6]

The history of the last hundred years has taught us to view such fervent certainty about a better world with skepticism, and Key's basic expectations of gender roles and the unimportance of educational institutions as no longer applicable. However, she was pleading the cause of the child in a new way at a time when the prevalent view was that the child was an important asset to the state. Childhood was assumed to be naturally akin to "a garden of delight" and, by being excluded from the world in general, a child should be able to develop "the habit of happiness" as a matter of course. The reality that most children did not have this opportunity was considered inconsequential. This was the world of implicit belief in the findings of science, and much advice was given on the avoidance of spontaneity, emotion and individualism in the rearing of children. A distance was prescribed fo parents between themselves and their offspring.

> The rule that parents should not play with their baby may seem hard, but it is a safe one. (United States Children's Bureau, 1914)

and

> There is one sensible way of treating children. Treat them as though they were young adults. Never hug and kiss them, never let them onto your lap. (John Watson, *The Psychological Care of Infant and Child*, 1928)

The child was to be inculcated with the virtues of self-control, obedience and respect for authority. A science-centered morality superseded the deity-centered morality of the previous century. Similarly, formula milk was promulgated as being preferable to breast-feeding because of its scientific reliability. Looking back on the formulations of that age, we can also realize how revolutionary Steiner was in his approach.

How is it, then, that at the end of the century our concern is, to use Postman's term, "The Disappearance of Childhood"? And why has the authoritative and confident tone, however lamentable the advice might seem to us now, given way to anxiety and doubts about our roles as parents, caregivers, and educators?

One cause is the greater awareness of the importance of childhood that has steadily manifested itself more and more strongly since the Romantic era at the beginning of the last century. Since World War II, the joy of parenting has been accompanied by a deep desire to "get it right." For this, parents need experts who advise them, even if this expert advice fluctuates and contradicts itself over time. In 1914, there were 175 pediatricians in the United States; by 1955 there were 6547, and this number doubled by 1966. We need expertise to help us with an ever more complex and demanding task and we set great value on our children's wellbeing.

In Shari L. Thurer's wonderfully readable and knowledgeable book *The Myths of Motherhood: How Culture Reinvents the Good Mother,* she describes this transformation. She believes that our hyper-empathetic ideal of parenting is partly a reaction to the loss of value accorded to human life in the 20th century as a result of genocidal events (such as the holocaust) and a greater awareness of child poverty and deprivation. In bringing up children, one idea supersedes another with bewildering speed, so that we always seem to be getting our awesome responsibility wrong.

> Few women could read about their formidable power to harm their children without a pang of conscience. What mother hasn't momentarily failed to stimulate or pay attention or delight in all

baby's accomplishments? Who hasn't been provoked by her children . . . screamed or even, dare I suggest, slapped them . . . only to undergo a black period of agonizing guilt and self-recrimination? According to child experts, even unconscious hostility could plant the seeds of neurosis in her offspring . . . A deficient mother (you!) could be exposed by the very symptoms of your child's pathology. Crankiness in a baby, withdrawal, uncontrollable crying, school phobia, surliness—all betray mother's ineptness.[7]

It is calculated that it costs £100,000 in the UK to bring up a child. Yet even in a society where such affluence exists, many children are undernourished, abused and deprived. On one side there is excessive consumerism. As the tide of an article in the *New York Times* once memorably put it: "It's a boy! It's a girl! It's time to shop!" In the United States, one in eight children goes hungry, and recorded abuse has increased by 40% since 1980. In the UK, child poverty has increased threefold since 1979, 350,000 children under age 12 are left daily in unsupervised homes, and 20% of children suffer from psychological problems, of which more than half are anxiety disorders.[8] These two countries are not exceptions in the Western world, as the problems are acknowledged as becoming more widespread. There are resistance factors that enable children to become what Norwegian researchers call "dandelion children," enabling them to cope with such disadvantages. These factors have been found to be good communication skills, a sense of religious faith, an ability to reflect and a strong attachment to parents in the first years. Yet many of our contemporary cultural trends tend to deny many children the possibility of developing these very abilities.

In all historical cultures there have been acceptable means whereby children could be transferred from biological parents to non-biological parents. For the ancient Celtic tribes of Britain, this transfer often took place when the child was seven years old, so that they would not become too circumscribed in one family setting and would develop skills of mobility and flexibility at a young age. In the last century, it was a method of family economic management whereby a family with too many mouths to feed could transfer a child to a family that needed another pair of working hands. Now it has become axiomatic that adults have the right to have a child as a source of their own emotional completeness. Society feels it is correct that childless couples are given this opportunity as a right to personal fulfillment. However, this attitude lands us with another tension on the question of bringing up children, where the area of human rights becomes entangled and self-contradictory.

As we saw at the beginning of the century, the essential vision of childhood was one of powerlessness and dependence, and good parenting prolonged this state. Now a hundred years later, the authority of parents has significantly declined and children demand and receive early access to the adult world. This is stressful for all concerned, and this tension works right down into the early years, as it affects the way we perceive our children. This signal is one to which they are acutely sensitive. A child is a person with rights and autonomy and yet also has the right to be a child. These two principles can be contradictory and therefore give rise to problems for us all. This right to be child is often expressed by its absence:

> Boredom!!! Shooting!!! Shelling!!! People being killed!!! Despair!!! Hunger!!! Misery!!! Fear!!! That's my life! The life of an innocent eleven year-old schoolgirl!!! A schoolgirl without a school, without the fun and excitement of school. A child without games, without friends, without sun, without birds, without nature, without fruit, without chocolate or sweets, with just a little powdered milk. In short, a child without childhood.[9]

As so often, what is absent becomes the definition of what an inviolate childhood should be.

In her seminal book *Children without Childhood*, Marie Winn looked at the radical changes taking place in the way adults were treating children and how this affected their behavior. Her concern was that parents were finding their traditional role as protectors of childhood more and more difficult to fulfill.

> [A]s today's children impress adults with their sophisticated ways, adults begin to change their ideal about children and their needs; that is, they form, new ideas about childhood . . . as adults act less protectively . . . and as they expose children to the underside of their, lives—adult sexuality, suffering, fear, of death—these former innocents grow tougher perforce, less playful and trusting, more skeptical—in short, more like adults.[10]

Winn sees this tendency as a regression to the Middle Ages, when there was no concept of protecting children from the exigencies of adult life. Following this came several centuries when childhood was seen as an estate clearly differentiated from adulthood. In Winn's view, it becomes vital, in an increasingly complex and turbulent society, to restore "real childhood," that the period of nurture and protection is not shortened, and that this needs adults to be encouraged to take an authoritative—but not authoritarian—role in family life.

However, it is not surprising that some parents, faced with a plethora of demands they feel ill-equipped to handle, and looking for simplicity in a confusing and contradictory task, find a more a authoritarian approach attractive. An example of this would be the organization Growing Families International, which has rapidly become a multi-million dollar business. Their publications recommend that babies as young as eight months should be drilled in high-chair manners, to sit up straight with their arms by their sides, and pinned in this position until they obey. At 18 months, babies should be smacked with a plastic spatula to "inflict pain, but not break bones or damage skin tissue." In a return to turn-of-the-century views, "Teach, the child to obey according to the character of true obedience, immediately, completely, without challenge and without complaint."[11] This flies in the face of the contemporary appreciation of each child as an individual and verges on child abuse, yet many parents resort to such ideas out of despair and not knowing where else to turn.

Paradoxically, this advice appears at the same time as another view suggesting that the parents have little influence on a child and that the most potent agents of child socialization are peer groups. Judith Rich Harris' paper,[12] which first appeared in *Psychological Review* in 1995, and her subsequent book *The Nurture Assumption*, has aroused much interest and her propositions have reverberated ever since. Like much else in this field, ideas generated in the United States wing their way across the Atlantic and become areas of debate and practice in Europe as well. Her convincing and well-written paper claims that, from the many hundreds of studies undertaken into parental influence on children, almost no evidence has come to light that proves this influence exists at all. Even evidence as to how children react to extreme experiences such as divorce, abuse and adoption are elusive because children react so differently. She points out that higher primates can be raised successfully by their peers when they have lost their mother, and she asks whether this could not also be the case with humans.

We swing from the omnipotent demanding parent on one hand to, on the other, the powerless parent who points to genetic traits, social pressures, consumerism, peer pressure, and birth order as being far more determinative of their child's development than they can be. Howard Gardner's effective critique of Harris' view, although showing respect for her sincerity and scholarship, shows that the peers a child has are basically a question of the society and circumstances the parents themselves create. There is a tremendous differentiation between cultures here. What applies in one setting need not apply to another, and the paucity of evidence for parental influence might be more due to a matter of a weakness in the scientific process, as there are certain elements of human life it does not take into account.

> In the absence of credible parents and other adults, most children would not be able to deal effectively with life ... Whether on the scene or behind the scenes, parents have jointly created the institutions that train and inspire children: apprenticeships, schools, works of art and literature, religious classes, playing fields, and even forms of resistance and rebellion. These institutions, and the adults who run them, sustain civilization and provide the disciplines—however fragile they may seem—that keep societies from reverting to barbarism.[13]

In other words, children are born into a culture and this culture, with all its assumptions, history and aspirations, will have a profound effect on how they experience their childhood and indeed their adult lives as well. Human cultures vary enormously in their approaches to the rearing of children, and one culture cannot claim to be the template of good practice for all.

Yet there is the factor of our common humanity and something that can be recognized as universal childhood. In our international work on behalf of the young child, we should strive to understand this, as well as to deepen our perception and knowledge of our own culture and others. In this roller-coaster-like plethora of advice, research and increasing polarization of views, we must look to the deeper aspects of childhood so that as parents, caregivers, and educators we do not also become restricted to a particular one-sided approach. The young child expects us to be social beings as well and will absorb from us our attitudes toward each other.

> How quality in early childhood education and care is defined and evaluated will be a concern not only for politicians, experts, administrators and professionals, but will also be a matter for a broader citizenry . . . It becomes important to create forums or arenas for discussion and reflection wherein people can engage with devotion and vision . . . Within these arenas a lively dialogue can take place in which early childhood education and care are placed within larger societal contexts and where questions concerning children's position are made vivid.[14]

If we wish to help our children develop "devotion and vision," we have to strive for them ourselves, as in our world they are no longer just a given fact of life. On this basis we can work for an international forum along the above lines and work in alliance with others who have goodwill towards the infant and young child for the benefit of children worldwide.

Universal childhood consists of basic elements that are a definition of being human and which appear in all our earliest years: the capacities for walking, talking and thinking. It is claimed that ninety percent of our learning takes place in the first three years of life, so how we learn these things is of fundamental importance to us all. Walking, for which we are biologically equipped, is nevertheless a cultural activity. The Wolf Children of Sri Lanka and the Gazelle Boy of the Sahara did *not* acquire this skill because they were brought up by the animals who adopted them as their own. Nor is it just a practical matter of locomotion, as these children who learned to run on all fours could be as swift as their animal associates.

> Underlying learning to walk there is an inner adjustment—an orientation of the young child. The equilibrium of the organism, with all its possibilities for movement becomes related to the equilibrium and all the possibilities for the movement of the whole universe, because the child stands within it. While learning to walk, children are seeking to relate their equilibrium to that of the entire cosmos. . . to meet the forces of statics and dynamics both in body and soul and to relate these experiences to the whole cosmos—this is what walking is all about.[15]

That these first steps are an enlightenment is vividly depicted on the child's countenance when it takes them. The child has found its place and beams up at us its joy at joining our community. In the ancient culture of Egypt, where these mysteries were experienced more directly and less cognitively, uprightness was divine. The backbone was venerated as the manifestation of the father god of the afterlife, Osiris. Mummy cases were made to stand upright for the passage through death, and uprightness was petrified and made immortal in the obelisk. One of the greatest yearly festivals was when a Djed column, the symbol of the backbone, was hoisted from a recumbent position to a vertical one; this was celebrated as a deed of resurrection. The child too experiences standing and walking for the first occasion as a unique and special event, towards which it has patiently struggled for some time.

Speech is likewise the accomplishment of the whole human being. For the last hundred years it was thought that the ability to produce speech was a function of particular areas of the brain. Recently, however, research has shown that there is a widely spread, multi-centered language system that extends through the whole brain, including areas that were previously thought to have nothing to do with it. It is therefore not just an additional skill that has been added in the course of evolution, but also something that permeates all our acts of thinking, feeling and remembering. Language flows out on the current of breath and provides a basis for our thoughts. An inviolate childhood is one in which these capacities are allowed to develop in such a way that they can be transformed and renewed later in life, not just as bodily functions but also as soul ones. A child must be allowed to breathe, in all the metaphoric and natural connotations of the word.

Martin Luther King stated: "We are challenged to rise above the narrow confines of our individualistic concerns to the broader concerns of all humanity . . . through our scientific genius we have made a neighborhood of our world; now through our moral and spiritual genius we must make of it a brotherhood." These are latent powers of childhood, and in respecting the early forms of these gifts in our caring and upbringing, we can help our children realize their potential later. What we learn, we learn so that we can transform it. We do not learn so that later we can be held in learning's thrall. Our first breath is an expression of our potential, just as our first cry is an expression of our rights on earth. For the Egyptians, breath was the manifestation of the goddess Isis. Unlike her consort, she remained on earth so as to accompany humankind in its destiny. Her wings were laid across the chests and lungs of the dead as they returned to the realm from which they had originally come. She lived in the air which we all share and united humanity by entering us all without exception or preference. She was wise beyond all measure because she alone knew the secret name of the sun god. In Egyptian art she is often portrayed holding the new child, the offspring of her marriage to Osiris, on her lap and giving him her breast. Steiner spoke of the need to find the new Isis, because we have lost her and because she is that which expresses our common humanity. In our realm of work with the earliest years of childhood, we can find that the wisdom of childhood informs and inspires us. We can work with the combination of Isis and Osiris and the incarnation of the child that is expressed by the *Sistine Madonna* in all its majesty.

> To this end it must really be so among us that one helps the other in love, so that a real community of souls arises in which envy and all such things disappear, and in which we do not each look at our own particular goal, but face together, united in love, the great goal we all have in common.[16]

This is the gift the child brings to us all, and in coming to a better understanding of this gift, and by giving it the time and space to unfold we are endeavoring also to transform ourselves.

Endnotes
1. Kjetsaa, G. *Fyodor Dostoyevsky: A Writer's Life*, New York: Macmillan, 1987.
2. Excerpts from "Prayer Before Birth" by Louis MacNeice, in *Selected Poems*, New York: Faber and Faber, 1964.
3. Steiner, Rudolf. *The Human Soul in Relation to World Evolution*, New York: Anthroposophic Press, 2001.
4. Family Aid Commission, Sweden, 1981, op. cit. *Transforming Nursery Education*, Moss and Penn, Chapman 1996.
5. *World Education Report*, UNESCO 1998, Table 1.
6. H. Cunningham, *Children and Childhood in Western Society Since 1500*, Longman, 1995.
7. Thurer, Shari L. *Myths of Motherhood*, New York: Penguin, 1994.
8. *Bright Futures. Promoting Children and Young People's Mental Health*, The Mental Health Foundation, 1999.
9. Filipovic, Z. *Zlata's Diary: A Child's Life in Sarajevo*, New York: Penguin, 1994.
10. Winn, Marie. *Children without Childhood*, New York: Penguin, 1984.
11. "Smack the Child and Praise the Lord," *The Independent*, September 24, 1999.
12. *Where Is the Child's Environment? A Group Socialization Theory of Development*, July 1995.
13. Gardner, Howard. "Do Parents Count?" *The New York Review of Books*, November 5, 1998.
14. Dahlberg and Åsen, *Evaluation and Regulation: A Question of Empowerment. Valuing Quality in Early Childhood Service*, Eds. Moss and Pence, London: Chapman Publishing, 1994.
15. Steiner, Rudolf. *The Child's Changing Conciousness*, New York: Anthroposophical Press, 1988.
16. Steiner, Rudolf. *The Search for the New Isis, the Divine Sophia*, Spring Valley: Mercury Press, 1983.

The Human Self

by

Karl Brodersen

translated by Ted Warren

Sometimes you meet people on the street whom you have not seen for a long time. Such coincidences are embarrassing when you find yourself trying to remember the name of the person who has engaged you in a conversation. Of course she knows you and your name, but you are pulling a total blank! Then, once you find the name, a series of memories pops up in your mind and you think to yourself: "How this person has changed!" Her eyes are the same, her smile is too, and eventually you find the relationship between the businesswoman standing before you now and the girl you took rowing along the fjord during the smooth spring evenings many years ago. Her hair is gray now, the beautiful face lined in wrinkles, and her voice is business-like due to her professional life. If your encounter were to turn into a conversation at a coffee shop, you might well observe outer signs that she has changed inwardly as well. The businesswoman has her own opinions on her friends, on the Prime Minister, on how to bring up children, and soon you realize that you have not rediscovered a friend, but actually lost one.

What is the shock about these meetings is not that the person has changed, we all do. She is the same person despite her changes. We can picture ourselves as babies, as children and then on through the stages of life with shifting features both inner and outer. We can imagine ourselves in our clothes from past years and the image becomes clearer. The shocking realization is that we have never been who we really are!

So we can ask: Who was she really? Who is this previous rowing partner and now-present businesswoman with four children and everything else that follows? If we look beyond the roles people play and the costumes they wear, what is there? The questions are not any different if we were to enter a deep psychological analysis of that human being, and consider which characteristics are intimate parts of the personality. They are subjected to the laws of change, and during our lifetimes we are recast many times. But the continuity, a feeling of unity remains from all the way back to our first memories. It was I who stood in the hall and burned matches when the angry women walked out, I, three feet tall with pants and big holes on my knees in the rust-brown homemade knee socks.

We can experience ourselves as the core of our conscious life, that which everything collects around, but we can also experience it in other people, for example when we discover them in new roles behind new masks. We say, "I" and thereby speak of the unique entity that lives in each human individual. That is certainly a paradox. Even if we investigate the "I" in us or in others more closely, we can shed the layers but still not find the core. Everything is in transformation, every quality we can attribute to a person can change and yet the person remains deep within her Self, for her consciousness and for the rest of us.

The Self is simultaneously the center and the periphery of our being. It feels like a core, but entails all of our qualities, experiences and relations to the world around us. The Self is a cohesive power that gives individual meaning to our lives. This power unites us more intimately with other people's Selfs, whether through sympathy, antipathy or neutral interest. In this way human beings are united not only geographically as dwellers on this limited planet, but they are united in their Selfs to one large entity, the whole of mankind. If we observe this from a more dynamic perspective by considering the Self both in its function and its development, we conclude that the Self not only includes who we *are* in the moment, but also who we *have been* and thereby provides continuity in our existence from the cradle to the grave. This feeling of identity with our Self through the shifting roles in life and on to broader feelings of identity with other people, yes, with all of humanity, is the only secure support for our existence.

When we hear little children repeat with grave seriousness something they heard from adults it seems comical or charming. Children unite themselves with words, with language but not with opinions. We can observe the same phenomena every day with adults who gossip about what others have said. However it is not as charming. The Self is not present in such outbursts, no matter how bombastically they are spoken. In sleep, in unconscious states of being, and under hypnosis, the Self completely removes itself from our words and our deeds. Similarly, it can also be more or less present in what we say and do. We can speak of a more or less state of Self. In English we cannot use the word *selfless* because it carries the additional meaning *unselfish*. We are defining a state of being where the Self is no longer active.

Another possibility is a state of being in which the Self becomes too strongly united with certain qualities or situations. The Self becomes fixated and egocentric because it loses its flow of transformation, its movement. Such obduracy, such callousness takes place in normal phases of personality development but it can also become a permanent state—with tragic consequences. Life is made up of continually new circumstances: friends shift, we age and truly meet new situations every day.

The deepest riddle of the Self is our destiny, the pattern in our lives and the coincidental events that receive meaning for us when placed together. These may be illnesses or emergencies, responsibilities or tasks, and it may be pleasant or unpleasant to meet the life that is our own, a part of our Self. Largely what we meet are the consequences of who we were previously and what we did. Some situations are so puzzling, so clearly incompatible with our earlier life that we might imagine we are meeting consequences from a previous life on earth.

The task of the Self is to unite itself with our entire existence and to receive the consequences of our own actions. A person who fails to do so loses his relationship with his inner being and either remains fixed in denial or defiance or flees from himself, in either direction abandoning the meaning of his life. We continually vacillate between these polarized possibilities.

I think it is important to point to true humanity, the entity in time and space because in our present time we employ great acumen to disconnect from our true being in its multiple factors, physiological, psychological and philosophical. The result of such endeavors is to release the human being from any responsibility for his actions. For example a crime can be explained away by factors of genetics and/or environment. The analysis may be accurate, but if we discount or remove a person's responsibility for his deeds, we also discount or remove part of his human dignity. As a prisoner said to me, "Of course there must be a punishment for crimes, but they should not be meaningless."

The Self that lives in us is threatened from many angles. Even in the societies where respect for the individual is strong, the modern technological ways of life challenge the Self to deal with situations it really cannot connect with. In our social life there is automation that prevents the Self from being present. Children struggle to adapt to the emptiness, meaninglessness, to the dehumanized activities surrounding them. The Self must adapt to the context it lives within but it is obliged to two sides of its being; it cannot abandon the entity nor the context in its being without being ruined.

A human being is never determined. It continually becomes something else, from the cradle to the grave, and as a core in the entire movement the Self retains the entity and the context, an entity and a context that tend to include more and more of the world we live in and to continue to include more people as if our lives depended on it!

The Free and the Unfree Spirit[1]

by

Ted Warren

translated by the author

By mentioning the capacity for moral intuitions, we touch upon a theme that is essential for any deeper understanding of the question of freedom. At the same time, this capacity in each individual is not easy to grasp and awaken. It is a field of knowledge that demands intense focus and repeated efforts. This capacity will not develop without difficulties as we are challenged to bring new consciousness into the course of our actions.

Every day we meet situations in life that are clearly influenced by mental pictures or experiences that are determined by past deeds. Many of these life situations present themselves as problems, for we realize that something has to change. We are forced to look at the problem in a new way, whether we want to or not. This is a complex situation, naturally, because not everyone sees the same problems, nor realizes the need for change.

In the individual life and in the world, many challenges arise out of the fact that personal and community activities are not longer able to develop naturally out of the given course of action. A quick glance through the newspaper will provide examples of unproductive and repulsive behavior: illusions of stability, the inordinate power of money, totalitarianism, first class weaponry, environmental ruin and many aspects of social life that no longer contribute to the health or positive development of a respective country. All of these problems are the result of past deeds and ways of life. And we are confronted with a major question: What do these problems have to contribute to the future? How will these challenges be transformed into positive aspects for the evolution of the human being?

Results of past deeds may be accompanied by a sense of emptiness. The human spirit is then placed behind a veil of helplessness and no one knows where to turn. The experience of this emptiness is something we share in common with all mankind. Such isolation may not be avoided, but more importantly is how we stand in this experience and work to create something new out of it.

We no longer receive moral impulses from the past. New moral impulses have to be sought for in the inner life of the individual, despite any obstacles created by past experiences or mental pictures. Through repeated efforts, the resistance is overcome and new strength of consciousness may be created by which the moral capacity for intuitions may be awakened. But how do we search? The given methods of natural scientific research may provide a valuable starting point, but they will not take us to the depth of the experience in the inner core of the individuality. Nor will passive behavior carry us very far. The many forms of materialistic mysticism that bring quick results may actually mask the true impulses working in the individual's life of soul. A genuine search for moral intuition is very hard work and will have to take place in the course of time. Our capacity for moral intuitions has to be discovered, actively employed and then strengthened day to day.

Let us look at the twofold nature of a free act of will. The first side may be seen in the spiritual activity that reaches the moral intuition. The activity of this intuitive element checks the human organism. This takes place when the free individual acts without external or internal influences, in such a way that the action is determined only by its ideal motive. The other side of the twofold nature is realized when the spiritual activity of the ideal element replaces the influences of the physical organism and works into the will.

The moral action must first take place and afterwards may the facts involved be understood. In this way our work differs from natural scientific research as we are not limited to the world of the senses and the motives for the deeds are not dictated by past deeds. If we first understand all the facts involved in an action, then these facts might be chosen as the motive for our action and thereby influence the possibility for a unique deed.

Various authorities from all walks of life may not see the possibility for a free act of will. They contend that no act of will may be free. And many people try to condition, manipulate or use individuals in order to gain advantage over them. Rudolf Steiner maintained that only those who cannot observe the twofold nature of a free act of will believe that free deeds are impossible. When we try to observe free acts of will, two qualities may build the basis for our observation. The first one is love for the action that is carried out. Thereby the free spirit is not bound by any duty or compulsion. And when this quality of love is strengthened over the course of time, the second quality may appear, namely, trust between those who are active together. Once the free action has been observed, new meaningful relationships between the free actions of other individuals may be researched.

We may take a step further in our search for new actions by examining the way in which the world of ideas works in two different people. In the social life we may find many examples of fixed orders that try to regulate or define the life of will of their people. On the other hand, we can find examples of individuals who merely seek the realization of their own egotistical needs. Neither type of activity can create the basis for a free social life.

How can two people experience the world of ideas in two different ways and still find a constructive way of working together in daily life? Before we approach a clear understanding of how ideas work in different people, let us look at Ralph Waldo Emerson's description of the world from which our intuitions spring:

> We denote this primary wisdom as intuition. In that deep force, the last fact, behind which analysis cannot go, all things find their common origin. For the sense of being, which in calm hours rises,

we know not how, in the soul, is not diverse from things, from space, from light, from time, from man, but one with them, and proceedeth obviously from the same source whence their life and being also proceedeth. We first share the life by which things exist, and afterwards see them as appearances in nature, and forget that we have shared their cause. Here is the fountain of action and the fountain of thought.[2]

If Emerson is correct in his observation, that the source of intuition is shared by mankind, and "not diverse from things," why do our experiences of that source differ? Why do we have individual moral intuitions and original deeds?

Steiner also observed the source of intuition—a world of ideas—as a unity, but unlike Emerson he went to great efforts to show how the ideas in this world of ideas become individualized through moral intuition. An action based on pure moral intuition does not have the perceptible content of the action as its motive. In other words, even though I may see the content of the action, I do not allow it to determine my action. If I allowed the content to determine the action, my action would not be free; it would be bound to that given content. When the motive for my action is determined by purely ideal activity, then the action is determined by the way in which the intuition works in my will at the actual moment of the activity. In this way two different people may have moral intuitions, but the contents of their actions do not interfere with the activity in the will that is determined by their unique intuitions. Both act freely and individually. We can observe Steiner's way of expressing a basis for free social life:

> A moral misunderstanding, a clash, is impossible between human beings who are morally free. Only the morally unfree who follow their natural instincts or the accepted commands of duty come into conflict with their neighbors if these do not obey the same instincts and the same commands as themselves. To live in love towards our actions, and to let live in the understanding of the other person's will, is the fundamental maxim of free human beings. They know no other obligation than what the will puts itself in unison with intuitively; how they will direct their will in a particular case, their faculty for ideas will decide.[3]

Free men and women must not necessarily agree with each other, as they realize that they conceive their ideas without obeying outer or inner authorities. Though their intuitions are individualized, they act together as one in spirit.

An unfree spirit first recalls past experiences in the form of mental pictures, and the motive for his actions accompanies the mental picture. He follows the given motive without creating original mental pictures. Perhaps an external authority intimidates him. Or he may have convinced himself to follow the decisions of a particular party line. He may feel bound to family traditions, or he may merely follow his blind instincts. In contrast, the free spirit uses his thinking to make an original decision. His motives are purely ideal, and he participates in creating new moral impulses.

That which we meet in the world of nature is given. Our new moral impulses, in contrast to the world of nature, must first be created. We have a necessary relationship to the moral laws of the past, but new moral ideas may not come from the past. Can educational systems designed in the past meet the needs of youth today? Am I justified in acting a certain way because so many people have done so in the past? Life changes after all, but do we?

Endnotes
1. This chapter is from *Freedom as Spiritual Activity* by Edward Warren, London: Temple Lodge, 1994.
2. Emerson, Ralph Waldo. "Self-Reliance," in *Essays*, Everyman's Library, London and New York: Dutton, 1995, p. 41.
3. Steiner, Rudolf. *The Philosophy of Freedom*, Chapter 9, London: Rudolf Steiner Press, 1979, p. 139.

Recapitulation (Recall) in the High School Main Lessons

by

Ken Power

Recapitulation or recall is the process of gathering together what has been achieved in the past day or days, so that a student can go forward in a more conscious manner. It establishes continuity and can lead to a growing understanding through comparison and experiencing change or development.

In main lesson the student engages in a process of active listening, responding and writing. The student's thoughts, feelings, and observations are written up for homework. The active listening and thinking, both in the lesson and the homework, engages the student's will and opens the soul to the enrichment of sleep. Significantly, recall allows a brief moment for this enrichment to come to consciousness. Often an essential idea not expressed in the course of the lesson or in the homework comes from sleep and will be stated the following day. If the whole class is listening carefully, the heart of the matter can be received by everyone while recalled by a student. Careful, active listening is of the utmost importance.

The high school main lesson is a balance of thought processes. It is beneficial to look at these processes as planetary qualities: Moon through Saturn. In Class 9 I have tended to concentrate on the first two of these qualities, Moon and Mercury. Therefore, careful, painstaking reproduction is required as well as the ability to observe in detail, list phenomena and make general comparisons. As the teacher I must insure a balance of qualities and inner dynamic by seeing that Jupiter and Saturn qualities are also present. If successful, the lesson will come alive of itself and not just out of the inspirational gifts of the teacher. Recall offers further opportunity for these latter qualities, Jupiter and Saturn, to come from the students themselves after having the space to sleep on the lesson.

For instance, after the lessons on Michelangelo in Class 9 History of Art, I have asked pupils to recall by writing in their notebooks the word or phrase which would sum up his work. Many students' hands shoot up and the words *will, purpose, courage* are spoken or rather called out. Some boys in the act of leaping out of their chairs give voice to not only a Saturn quality in the word *will* but a Jupiter quality in the leap.

As mentioned above, the main lesson should contain a variety of thought processes in dynamic interaction. This dynamic should be fostered in each part of the main lesson in metamorphosis. We can therefore look at each of the six planetary qualities, the three below the Sun—Moon, Mercury and Venus—and the three above—Mars, Jupiter and Saturn—in relation to recall as an essential part of the main-lesson. Below I will give examples of recall which have worked in main lesson and which stimulate a given thinking (planetary) quality.

First is Moon, the ability to remember and reproduce or repeat something accurately. A written description in a given time of, say, ten minutes, of a painting, a part of a biography, a story, a route taken, an experiment are examples of this form. A sketch of a painting detail or a map would be another approach. More examples and variations can be used and made suitable to different classes.

Next is Mercury, the making of comparisons and concise lists of relevant points. Here I have often asked students to compare two subjects, either two paintings from one main lesson or two paintings of the same period but different artists, or two works of art from different periods. Sometimes I will ask students to look only for similarities, at other times only differences. Possibilities are almost endless, but careful attention needs to be paid to what is asked of each age group.

The last "under Sun" quality is Venus, the realm of feeling, and here the feelings of the pupils need to be taken as objective phenomena and thought about. Sympathy and antipathy with respect to a painting, a story or an animal species are facts as much as the red of a robe or the blue of a crystal. Class 10 marks a good beginning time to teach this and the recall in a clear, precise manner of one's feelings; and the attempt to designate these properly is an excellent exercise. It is very good for vocabulary work as well.

The fourth quality is Mars, the forming and expression of sound judgment based on sound reasoning. Various recall exercises can encourage this. In the Friday lesson the students can be asked to recall the whole of the week in reverse order. In Class 11 they can be asked to recall three subjects from each day in reverse order as well as the above. This is more than remembering. It is establishing a right order, which is more difficult. The teacher needs to have thoroughly prepared for this one, or he/she will be caught out. Next, the teacher can take any recall exercise, as above or below, but ask a pupil to come forward and read his own recall (Classes 9/10) or speak it extemporaneously (Classes 11/12). This speaking out in front of the class is a Mars quality and, as such, should be done properly—standing straight, speaking slowly and clearly, not dropping words, and so forth. The reading out of homework is also helpful in this regard. In my lessons, every student has the opportunity to stand in front of the class and read his/her homework essay. The shy ones are helped because they know everyone has to do it; it is taken seriously, the class is appreciative and it has "always been done."

In Class 11, they can begin to criticize each other's essays. The teacher must be sensitive here but the students need and even want this. It must be well structured, clear and simple. The criteria of criticism need to be well defined and easily understood. For example, the teacher could ask the class to note the number of physical qualities, colors, objects, and so on, noted by the reader with respect to a given painting. Based on this, the teacher could then ask if a full enough description was given. Students can also take one of their own sketches (Classes 9–12) and critically compare it with the original, following clearly stated criteria. In Classes 11 and 12, they can perform the above with a sketch from another classmate. Both critiques, as well as all the above recall exercises, are written up and included in the main lesson book.

Jupiter gives the opportunity to recall gesture, the dramatic gesture of a lesson, a period, a sculpture, and so forth. In the Class 9 History of Art lesson, I have asked a class to close their eyes and recreate the image of, say, the painting *Madonna of the Rocks* by Leonardo da Vinci, and then to picture clearly the Madonna, her hands, posture, head, and so on. One student is asked to come to the front and recreate the Madonna's exact position. Other students can come forward and alter this, the first student becoming the model for the day until the class is satisfied. The teacher does not have to show the slide or print to check for accuracy. Working on the gesture is the important thing.

Finally, Saturn is the essence of what we do and what we strive to think about. We sacrifice hours of time and effort for this quality, and it is worth the sacrifice. The students make the sacrifice willingly. But what is it? And, more importantly, can the pupils find it in themselves? Earlier in this essay I mentioned this quality in connection with a main lesson on Michelangelo. I asked the students to recall the one word or phrase which would sum up his work. The teacher could also ask for three words, or a sentence, to characterize a work, a life, and a period. In Class 11 students have discovered the meaning of style in this manner.

Recall in main lesson can be used to encourage, indeed to train, a moral, living thinking in students. Although only a small part of a main lesson, the whole array of thinking qualities can be found within recapitulation and used as a teaching tool.

THE ODYSSEY OF CONSCIENCE[1]

by

Henning Andersen

a book review by Oddvar Granly
translated by Ted Warren

We all have memories from our childhood of the first time we were confronted by our conscience. For example, of the time when a tempting cake stood on the table while Mom and Dad were out in the kitchen; we had a guilty conscience but the cake sure tasted good! Or of the other time when our inner voice spoke and we helped a friend. Looking back we notice that we became aware of such feelings at a certain point in time, that the feeling of conscience had not always been there, it appeared.

This leads us to ask when conscience appeared in the evolution of mankind. Can we point to the moment of creation of conscience and trace the phases of development through which it has passed? Waldorf teacher Henning Andersen asked himself these questions and wrote up his results in a book titled *The Odyssey of Conscience*. One of his tasks was to illuminate conscience and the developmental phases of the concept of conscience in ancient times based on texts from Homer, Aeschylus, and Euripides and on passages from the New Testament: St Paul and parts of the four Gospels. His other task was to edit Rudolf Steiner's descriptions of the appearance of conscience in ancient times and its relationship to mankind's development since then.

A number of middle-Europe authors have written from an anthroposophical perspective on the transformation of consciousness and have spoken of the emergence of conscience in Greece in the fifth century BC. Ernst Uehli, Emil Bock and Friedrich Hiebel addressed this in their cultural-historical works. The strength of Andersen's book is its breadth in the presentation of conscience as specific phenomena. The reader notices that Andersen's insights into the Greek tragedies are the fruit of many years of dedicated study of and loyalty to the works—to the extent that, behind the poetic words, the spiritual dimensions have spoken.

The following example from his book is his descriptions of Aeschylus' play *Eumenides* [The Furies]. When Agamemnon returns from Troy, he is murdered by his wife Clytemnestra and her lover Aigisthos. His son Orestes seeks revenge and kills them both:

> It is worth noting that Orestes' experiences are almost removed of anything we would call the pains of conscience. He is moved emotionally by what he sees but more in the way we are filled with

fear when we face something threatening. He knows that the beings before him represent 'revenge in the form of a pack of hounds, sent by his mother,' but the experience does not reach his inner life to awaken regret or desperation from his actions. He is shook up but not about himself.

It has been said that the scene in which Orestes sees Erinyes come storming over him is a description of the pangs of human conscience. With the help of symbols for the sake of dramatic effects, Aeschylus gives conscience the outer trappings of the goddesses of revenge.

Had something similar happened to Aeschylus, he would certainly never have been accused of unveiling the secrets of the mystery centers in Greece. He was taken to court because in him lived an individual with the resonance of earlier initiation. Because Aeschylus knew the effects of ritual murder and knew what the executer was exposed to and which forces confronted him in the moment of murder, he could describe the stages that Orestes experienced when he killed the murderers. Orestes receives insight into the world of godly beings to which everyone else is still blinded. He is driven out by the powers that he sees clearly. He must leave the scene from one moment to the next as if he were forced by the threat of weapons.

Here Aeschylus does not work with symbols but with realities, just on another level than the chorus leader. If the reader takes this into account, he can meaningfully place *Eumenides* in the timeline of the development of human consciousness. Aeschylus knows that there are two kinds of people: those who still have spiritual experiences and those who no longer have them. If the reader postulates that Aeschylus uses symbolic language, then he will forget or ignore this relationship and thereby miss the value of his works. We will revisit the question of symbolic language later on.

While in the last part of *Oresteia* the Chorus consists of Furies, the goddesses of the sea, in the first part, the Chorus consists of old men whose attention was directed to the past from which came all instruction for their actions. They honored the old gods and maintained the old traditions. As Cassandra warned what would soon take place around them they could not understand her words, and when the events transpired, they were totally crippled in their willpower, which left them able merely to create *thoughts* on what they *should* do. They were subjected to the necessities of the past and did not know the free forces of initiative for the future.

In *The Choephori* the Chorus consists of captured women from Troy who suffer daily from the ruling pair (Clytemnestra and Aigisthos), and by their words and actions lent strength to Orestes and Pylades toward their goal. Simultaneously, in their inner lives they painfully empathize with Orestes in his reaction to the murders.

In *Eumenides* the Chorus consists of entitled people, which design provides an indication of where we are today. The weight is placed in the world of the gods, which also confirms at first sight the cast list: in addition to Orestes and Eumenides, we find the ghost of Clytemnestra, Apollo, Athena and a priestess of Apollo's Temple in Delphi. The priestess is an oracle, a being with access to the spiritual world. She is able to see the goddesses of the sea among the people immediately surrounding Orestes after the murder of Clytemnestra. By itself the cast list takes us beyond the earthly world. For that same reason Pylades does not appear in the third part of the trilogy. Even his closest friends are not allowed to take such a journey that will not avoid the gods.

That means, at the same time, that this is not the day-to-day Orestes we meet in *Eumenides*, but a far more significant Orestes that Aeschylus points to at the end of *The Choephori*:

> Next came a hero's kingly sufferings, and stabbed in a bath the warrior Chieftain of the Greeks perished. Now two once more, third in order, there hath come, we know not whence, a savior, or should I call it doom? Where then is the violence of calamity, when lulled, to find an end; or where is it to reach a termination?

Thus Aeschylus lets us know that the essential questions for the Greeks of his day were: What is the relationship between family and the individual? Shall one murder draw the next one with it into eternity? Can there not be redemption from this eternal cycle? Cannot an evil cycle be broken? In brief, here is how these themes play out in *Eumendides*:

Orestes seeks the temple at Delphi to receive the protection of Apollo. He is promised it and is cleansed of his guilt by the god who suggested he kill Agamemnon's murderers. He is sent to Athena and Hermes, who is not only the god of all travelers but also the guide of souls to the underground.

The ghost of Clytemnestra rises and awakens the sleeping Erinyes so they can resume their persecution of Orestes. Erinyes and Apollo exchange words, and, with his bow, Apollo drives the women, dressed in black, out of the holy place.

In Athens the goddesses of the sea find Orestes as he clings in supplication to the statue of Pallas Athena. They sing their magic songs and dance their round dance to lame his soul and ice his stomach before he is to be buried in his grave. Athena arrives in time to take the situation in hand—she calls in the parties to argue their cases at the newly-appointed court on the Ares heights, the Areopagos. After hearing both sides Athena rules to acquit Orestes; it is settled in his favor. Cleansed of guilt and free of persecution, Orestes is allowed to return home, and he leaves the court, accompanied by Apollo.

Athena remains behind with a flock of furious Erinyes to whom she immediately offers a home under her temple at the Acropolis. She bestows on them the honor to promote joy at home, in the fields, among the animals and in each mother's womb. Thus the Erinyes were transformed into friendly Eumenides.

It has often been pointed out that Aeschylus's intention with *Eumenides* was to show that the horrors of bloody revenge that ravage families could be replaced by the power of justice served by a court of volunteers. Such a court shall have the authority to set passions aside and put a stop to its free reign. This perspective belongs to an evaluation of the drama, especially from the perspective of conscience when one considers how in modern times there is a relationship between society's judgments and punishing mandates and the resulting experience of conscience in the inner life of man.

But to consider this the main message which Aeschylus brought to his time is a mistake. The substitution of justice for bloody revenge has significant effects on the transformation of the human soul structure. It is effects and transformations that are the main subjects of Aeschylus' works. Therefore Orestes cannot remain in the physical world; he must delve deeper or climb higher to find them. He enters the underground to the Erinyes and reaches up to Olympus with its gods, and his task in *Eumenides* is to arrange a confrontation between the gods and the sea goddesses so soul constitution of the human being can be classified.

In that context let us view a key passage, the scene in which Apollo and Orestes meet on the Areopagos together with the Erinyes, who proceed to ask Orestes about the murder of his mother. The accused does not deny the murder and explains how it occurred but mentions Apollo's incentive role in it. He asks his accused a question: Why did they not pursue Clytemnestra after she killed Agamemnon?

The Greeks who experienced these tragedies already knew the answer. Everything that came down through the ages, their entire inheritance that was firmly settled in their inner feelings pointed in a certain direction: Clytemnestra did not kill her own blood, but even worse were the crimes Orestes committed. Therefore it must have shaken the sensitive audience in the Theater of Dionysus to their bones to hear Orestes's reaction:

The Erinyes:
　The man she murdered was not of the same blood.
Orestes:
　Am I connected with my mother by the bands of blood?
The Erinyes:
　Yes, blood hound! Under her heart your mother bore you. How
　can you deny blood's valuable inheritance?

One must imagine that Orestes asks his question not only to the Erinyes but to himself. The insight he gained from Apollo at Delphi and under his torment after the murder is so new to him and mysterious that he continually asks himself how he is truly connected with other humans. Orestes notices to some extent the connection with relatives through blood. Inside he acknowledges a memory of family that allows him to look backwards from generation to generation. He knows deep inside that he has his father's being in him as well as his grandfather's being. But he also notices a new element from one side that has grown stronger and stronger through the generations: the experience of an isolated individual and a new organ for knowledge that has slowly replaced the capacity to observe the world of the gods as a picture.

When he searches for this element among his forefathers, he finds his father's (Agamemnon's) much too thoughtful, unpurified image of himself. He sees it clearly, and he finds it in all previous generations of his family, all the way back to Tantalus, who sacrificed his own son, tore apart his life content to control the godly clairvoyance with the power of thinking, and for which he was severely punished because the evolution of thinking cannot take place simultaneously with the evolution of clairvoyance.

Through blood Orestes is related to his family; but through this new consciousness, thinking isolates him within himself, just as it isolated Tantalus. The isolation and his thinking help him discover an inner core of being that was previously hidden by the family experiences and the world of picture images. While today we say, "He cannot see the forest for the trees"—the details prevent us from seeing the totality—in earlier times, it was just the opposite: One did not see the trees for the forest. In other words an all-encompassing picture consciousness separated us from the individual, both in the outer world and in the inner. For the Tantalus family, the individual experience appeared bit by bit, and simultaneously a growing need to remove the isolation and reconnect with the world that was now lost for them. This need combined with the wish to once again eat at the table of the gods, to reconnect with their forefathers, to meet their mothers and to experience the totality of life. But the totality was broken and the new totality complex, but still a totality, for one will be conscious within it, acting consciously and loving consciously. A new contact with the world is possible but the pathway may be navigated only by thinking and by new powers of love from individual to individual. It will no longer be navigated by families and blood relationships, but with consciousness—from Orestes to his father—and it will be aimed at the individual Agamemnon, and also from Orestes to the individual Clytemnestra.

Therefore the question of knowledge becomes: Am I connected with my mother by the bands of blood? From that ancient view Orestes answers for himself: "Yes, blood hound! Under her heart your mother bore you. How can you deny blood's valuable inheritance?"

Yes, he can. The old world order based on ancient families of gods is over. A new one has begun, and if one asks it for advice, he will experience new values because the balance of the world has been moved. And when the question is asked: How can we defy the inheritance of valuable blood relationships?, an answer appears from the new world order. Therefore, at this precise moment Orestes turns to Apollo. He prays to the god to explain to the Erinyes if his mother died "justifiably or not."

With Apollo's appearance we see that his disgust for Orestes' persecutors is stronger than his arguments, but if you take his comments as indications of the deeper basis upon which Aeschylus' tragedy rests and not as witness documents in an intellectual, legal process, everything looks different.

Apollo points out that, as a prophetic god, he does not lie but always proclaims what Zeus, the father of all gods, asks of him. Many answers have been given from the oracle at Apollo's holy temple at Delphi—to many cities that have asked for advice when in danger, and also to the countless individuals who sought guidance in their daily activities. Characteristic of the answers—and we have records of many—was always their ambiguity. I am not searching for any weakness in the "art of prophesy," but for a meaningful characteristic of the family of the gods to which Apollo belongs.

Apollo descended from a family of gods that arose from violent battles with earlier families of godly beings. First Chaos ruled, which has nothing immediately to do with the word as we use it today but was a world of archetypal images waiting to be realized in physical form. From that world of latent, spiritual, creative forces arose a family of gods that formed a totality: Uranus and Gaia, the heavenly and the earthly principles. Their descendents were the Titans, six male and six female. Fearing they would rob him of his power, Uranus threw the Titans down to Tartarus, the deepest realm of the underworld.

Gaia forged a steel sword and gave it to her youngest son, Chronos, who, in his outrage over the fate of the Titans, mutilated his father. Of Uranus' blood arose not only the Giants but also the Erinyes. Therefore it is not hard to understand that the sea goddesses had blood forces violently housed within.

From the Titans, Chronos and Rhea became the next family of the gods. Chronos liberated his sibling Titans and married his sister Rhea, who gave birth to Pluto, Poseidon, Zeus, Demeter, Hestia and Hera. Chronos also feared his own children when it was prophesied that one of his sons would take away his power. Therefore he swallowed them as they were born. Only the youngest son, Zeus, did not suffer that fate when his mother immediately placed a stone in the birthing clothes and tricked Chronos into swallowing it instead of the newborn. Zeus was taken to Crete and hidden in a grotto on Mt. Ida and nourished by bee honey, goat milk and ambrosia brought to him by doves.

But Zeus' siblings once again saw the light of day because Rhea tricked Chronos into drinking a poison. Zeus joined his siblings, took power from Chronos, and banished him to Tartarus together with the other Titans. He set guards on them so they would never return. Zeus became the head of the third family of gods, consisting of the six children of Chronos and his own children: Pallas Athena, Ares, Hephaestus, Apollo, Artemis, Aphrodite and Hermes.

By this time human beings had already existed for some while. Uranus and Gaia had created them when they created the world. When humans stood before Zeus, they did not stand before their creator but before a god who was himself created and could recall the family of gods that preceded him and had fought with each other. Even Zeus' fight for power lived in his memory. So we have a family of gods who came from a lineage and have the capacity for remembering, and from many avenues this capacity was given to the humans in the form of clear thoughts, reflections and recollection.

For hundreds of years Delphi was the main seat of learning and advice from the world of the gods. Often the prophecies were ambiguous but within their mystery lay hidden intention that was aligned with the key task of this third family of the gods—to challenge mankind to not only "Know Thyself" but to "Know Thyself in the World." In addition to the advice from the gods, the petitioner received help to increase his own power of knowledge.

The Greeks loved the clear light of day and therefore also insight and wisdom. Above them, their gods carried the task of promoting clarity of thought; they lived high up on Mount Olympus and reveled in the light of day.

In contrast, the Greeks resisted darkness and everything that was darkened and impenetrable. Death was for them something to dread. In Hades humans led a life in shadow and in death were themselves transformed to shadows, from which light was always hidden; from the kingdom of death one never returned. The gods of the underworld were surrounded by brooding darkness that traveled inside the earth or in the under-conscious forces of man and lived in his blood and in the collective, family ties, as well as darkened states of consciousness. To these gods belong the Erinyes who arose from the blood drops of Uranus.

In the scene in *Eumenides* when these beings of darkness stand before Apollo, we see these two opposing factions of the gods standing in the battle for the human being, an old being but of significance to the gods because it has the ability to change. When Apollo expresses that he does not lie in his own activities and prophecies and instead defers to Zeus, he speaks with clear words about what the battle for the human being means: Shall he go down to the under-consciousness and purge his experience of Self or should he pursue the activities of thought and knowledge? In ancient language: Shall he move to the mother principle or the father principle?

Thus the dialog exposes the conflicting relationships between the underworld and the supernatural gods, between the old and the new, between blood and nerve, conflicting relationships that appear both in men and women, implanted by the first family of gods, Uranus/Gaia, the forces of heaven and earth.

Yet this family of gods was creative. Zeus observes, judges and works with wisdom. Therefore when Agamemnon is murdered, the new element of thinking is also "murdered" and, even though it is unpurified in Agamemnon, it is that which shall be saved for the future. Aeschylus works with this point of view in his trilogy. He has the outraged Erinyes to protest that Zeus misused the father principle when putting his father Chronos in irons. Apollo's reaction is filled with anger and disgust:

> Ah ye abominable, brutish, god-detested! Fetters he may loose, for that there is remedy; and many, very many are the means of undoing what is done. But when the dust hath swallowed the blood of mortal man, once he is dead, there is no raising of him. Spell for this, none hath my father made; all else without breath of displeasure, this way, or that again, he doth reverse and dispose.

With his thoughts Zeus can turn things inside out. This is part of the opportunity that thinking provides but also its shadow. In relation to death Zeus is powerless. Death is shadow as well. But there is a great difference between sending Chronos to the kingdom of death and to Tartarus. Apollo argues that Chronos retains the option to transform, to loosen his chains and leave the underworld where the Erinyes live. He can raise himself to the father principle. Whereas if he were in the kingdom of death, all hope would be gone.

Apollo points to the world that is created around the third family of gods, the future world. His speech would sound like pure caprice if it were not seriously connected to the question of consciousness. For we must realize that the ancient Greeks understood the speech and the themes presented in the Dionysos performances. They experienced godly forces in the characters of Zeus and Pallas Athena, not only in their surroundings but also deep within their souls. For them the picture images were clear indications of the realities they experienced intensely. They went to the theaters not to be entertained, but to learn. And through enlightenment they experienced catharsis.

> This, too, I will explain, and mark thou how straightforwardly. The mother of what is called her child—is no parent of it, but nurse only of the young life that is sown in her. The parent is the male, and she but a stranger, a friend, who if fate spares his plant, preserves it till it puts forth. And I will show thee a proof of this argument. A father may become such without a mother's aid. Here at my hand is a witness, the child of Olympian Zeus—who even ere she came to light, grew not in any womb, yet is a fairer plant than all the powers of heaven could beget.

Zeus took Metis, wisdom, as his first wife. Though fate decided Metis should bear him a son who would be the king of the gods and of human beings, he swallowed his wife. Afterwards he felt pregnant and Pallas Athena was born from his head after Hephaestus as midwife chopped a hole in his forehead. Athena sprang from the opening in full armor swinging a sharp lance. The goddess of thoughtful intelligence and peaceful superiority, Athena is also the patron for the arts and handicrafts, being an expert weaver herself. She taught humans how to weave threads together with well-ordered and harmonious methods, both with physical materials and with the life of thinking.

It is Pallas Athena and Apollo who lead Orestes to victory. And Apollo appeals to the Erinyes to look to the future human being and not remain stuck in the powers of blood and family that merely hold humans in the past. Both work with the significance of thinking in human life, one in the direction of wisdom, intelligence, goodness and inner balance, the other in the direction of enthusiasm, transferring cosmic light through purified power and healing forces. Both fight darkness and support forces for the individual. And both have the task of liberating human beings from the underworld and demonic powers.

But the battle to be fought is not for the humans in the first phase, it starts with the gods. In Aeschylus' drama, the individual forces in mankind are not yet fully developed. Therefore we experience in Orestes no inner battle and no pangs of conscience from his bloody deeds. Rather, the battle rages on a supernatural level: Apollo and the Erinyes are fighting for the humans. The underworld wants to imprison them within blood relationships and in the collective depth of family under-consciousness, while Apollo wants to raise them to the level of knowledge, independence and responsibility.

And when Apollo advises Orestes to murder not his "mother" but rather the "murderer of Agamemnon," this is not a capricious method for dealing with a difficult problem but a precise characterization of the core of the saga. Orestes shall not necessarily murder his mother, but fight the forces that want to destroy the manly principle, the awakening consciousness and the youthful thinking. This occurs by restricting the attack on the individual by the forces of blood and family. From this perspective the death of Agamemnon was a greater catastrophe than the death of Clytemnestra.

And yet it was necessary that Agamemnon was murdered or that part of his being was destroyed. He had sacrificed his own daughter in Aulis and called out the outrage from the underworld to which Clytemnestra was connected. He had within himself the new possibilities for mankind but in unpurified form. Therefore he was forced to leave the future task to his children.

In the drama *Orestes* we witness Orestes beginning to take the very first steps upon the path of conscience. This occurs in *The Choephori* when Orestes asks Pylades if they shall pardon the murderers but Pylades immediately prevents him from falling out of his secondary role by pointing to the true owner of the main role: "Where, then, are the oracles of Apollo uttered at Python and the faithful oaths well plighted? Deem all thine enemies rather than the gods." In other words: Hold yourself to your higher being rather than your lower. This spiritual-soul constellation should very soon undergo a radical transformation in history.

But for now the gods do battle and the human beings are merely passive participants. Described fifty years later by Euripides in a different soul-suffering manner, the battle in the case of Aeschylus occurs at a world level above the human capacity. Orestes explains to Apollo that he *had* to murder his mother. Just before that he asks the Erinyes why they did not persecute Clytemnestra—the very same question Apollo asked the same beings. This question points to the main problem in *Orestes* and also to the projection from the gods to human beings.

The gods experience in advance and work through what human beings are later exposed to once their consciousness is developed to the extent they can work with the challenges. Therefore Apollo accompanies Orestes when he leaves the scene after the judgment is handed down after Athena's decisive vote.

The judges balance each other. Their presence in the play is background; they do not speak nor are they listed in the cast. We approach their world to give them an important task but remain on the supernatural plane.

We are in the world of the gods where Athena remains with the Erinyes, beings of the underworld that she first defeated in their fight for Orestes and which she later transforms in their inner beings so they become the Eumenides, the positive ones who live at her temple at the Acropolis.

The way is paved and the scene is cleared for a game that will soon take place not in the supernatural world, where gods fight with gods while humans are passive participants, but on the inner human plane, where the gods are interested and positive observers or participants from the sidelines. Human beings can now learn in their soul world to fear the inner voice more than "the world's severe judgments," where an inner rage slowly replaces the "god's rage."

* * *

Henning Andersen deepens our background understanding of consciousness through explaining Odysseus' experiences, on his ten-year homeward journey from Troy to Ithaca, as stages in the path from atavistic clairvoyance to an awakening in individual thinking that enables the individual to take responsibility for his deeds. The Cyclops represents ancient clairvoyance:

> The Cyclops has one eye and with that eye he cannot see sharply, in detail or judge distances. It is the clairvoyant eye and it sits in the middle of the forehead as it did with Goliath. In both cases they were destroyed so the new human with two fixate eyes could emerge. It is a precise description of the transition to the new state when Homer allows Odysseus to call himself Nobody. Then Polyphemus is blinded and described as the being who can no longer judge outer distances: first he throws too far and then too short.
>
> One thing Odysseus and Polyphemus have in common is a lack of conscience. Understandably, Polyphemus does not have it; he has neither the necessary individualization process nor the necessary thinking. He is older than both Apollo and Pallas Athena. He lives in his environment with his lambs and goats. He loves them with the warmth of his blood. His poetic conversation with his dear ram when Odysseus leaves the cave grips our hearts and makes it difficult for us to believe that this is the same creature who earlier smashed Greek skulls against the cliffs, which act did not disturb him. For him the world is simple.
>
> But it is unnatural for Odysseus to have no conscience. Nor is it acceptable that he first blinds Polyphemus and then yells demeaning words from a safe distance. Thinking and reflecting have become active in him and soon he will follow another's advice because of his conscience.
>
> Odysseus is a person who is in the transition from the old to the new form of existence. His thinking has reached the point where he can carry on conversations with Athena and also make his own decisions. He can move freely from his own world of thoughts to the

gods. Despite his ability to think, he can still see godly beings. This is due to his initiation and the entire *Odyssey* is a detailed description of the path of initiation for an individual who can think and thereby attain separation from the spiritual world while fighting his way back to a reunion with that world as a more highly-developed being.

But Homer (circa 853 BC) lived at an earlier time than Euripides (480 BC), and that is significant:

> With Homer we do not reach the concept of conscience, but rather a feeling of shame. This is the decisive difference. To have shame is a reaction in the soul to actions that are not only observed on the outside but also on the inside. We are confronted with a Self that is placed in an environment. But in that moment when the experience is not only *experienced* but also *discovered*, there is the basis for conscience. A consciousness exists with something that is itself.

Just as the Erinyes spoke from the outside to the Ancient Greeks, the laws spoke to the Jewish people and God revealed himself to Moses in the thorn bush. Andersen proposes that the coming of Christ created a new relationship that he called "the Christian internalization." Conscience is absolutely a part of the development of the Self. It begins speaking from the inside when the Self is strengthened, but the Self finds its full development only when it unites with the Christ impulse. Henning devotes a significant part of the book to St Paul and Judas. Two very different fates are described:

When St Paul acknowledged, from his own experience, that Christ was incarnated in Jesus, he received the most encompassing experience of conscience. He experienced the joining of the highest spiritual with the deepest human. This phenomenon responds to the lower and higher selves in individual human beings that we define as conscience. He experienced the constellation that was prophesized for hundreds of years. These are the forces that worked from the past and created the basis for historic descriptions of conscience, of which we have described a few.

The book gives us a solid description of conscience, which we are happy to receive from a landsman of Søren Kierkegaard's.

Endnote
1. Henning Andersen, *The Odyssey of Conscience,* Copenhagen: Hernov Forlag Denmark. 1996.

War and Peace and Moral Imagination

by

Oskar Borgman Hansen

translated by Ted Warren

War was once an instrument for deciding important disagreements between sovereign states. War was not considered a very practical method, but it did provide legitimate evidence for both parties, even the losing one. The loser, considering the loss merely a temporary decision, could seek revenge, merely. Within the surrender there was also a physical necessity. Despite the devastation, war was carried out with a certain decorum, a respect for the enemy. Parties seldom fought to annihilate the enemy. They fought to achieve particular goals: conquer a city, a harbor, or land, or carry out a demand for inheritance or to enjoy trade advantages. The victor had no motivation to continue the fight once his goal was reached. There were not wars that were concluded as World War II was, with the overreaching demand by the Allies that the Germans surrender unconditionally, a demand that struck at the German government, itself a non-Nazi government.

An example of mutual respect despite bitterness is the War of 1864 between Denmark and Prussia and Austria. The prize to the victors was the duchies—and solely the duchies. As Prussia's war goals did not include parts of the kingdom, for practical reasons they were willing to pay reparations to Denmark for the areas added to the peace agreement. The reparations included eight areas near Kolding just south of the old border between the kingdom and the duchies.

Few people understand the message of peace in the Gospels that calls for an immediate end to war as a means for deciding disagreements between states. Instead, they find religious justification for war, and the warring parties are mutually convinced that the final outcome will be blessed by God, that His *will* will be revealed in the historical changes of victory and defeat for the people. However, today war between civilized countries is meaningless as a means to achieve limited goals or decide matters of religion.

A German war propaganda phrase used during World War I was: "God punish England." An empty phrase—just as empty as the Allies' attempt to disguise their true goal by claiming that they had to protect Belgium's neutrality. Today a war would have to be fought based on an inner lie. We can ask: For which goals do we fight wars today, to protect territory or rights?

At the beginning of World War II, the Allies watched Hitler take over Czechoslovakia. After a year of allowing him to expand his kingdom at the expense of smaller kingdoms, the Allies were extremely anxious when they realized they needed a total crusade to remove the danger Hitler brought to mankind. Yes, Nazism was a threat to mankind, an expression of barbarism the likes of which we had never seen before. Had the Western countries acted with this conviction sooner, as early as 1933, there never would have been a second World War.

After many mistakes we have learned that dictatorship must be stopped by military action. There is no point in further discussion about what to do, what needs to be done once a situation has reached such a crisis. No other course seems possible, only military action remains. But to prevent such a situation from developing in the first place, moral attitudes are essential. Here is where communism differs from Nazism: Its followers do not try to take over power by attacking new countries; rather, they occupy them from within.

All responsible people and almost all responsible politicians in every country want peace today and if we doubt that, we do not trust their motives. We do not know which conditions they will eventually accept for choosing war in a crisis, and we have every reason to doubt that they have the ability to sustain everlasting peace. Therefore their actions are greatly influenced by fear as well as "national egotistical" or "regional egotistical" interests.

Peace can be accomplished when we understand how to fight spiritual battles with spiritual resources and when we have a perspective that views mankind's interests at large, not merely our own personal or group interests. True peace, not just the condition where there is no war. Three hundred years ago Baruch Spinoza, Dutch rationalist and philosopher (1632–1677), wrote: "If a state and its people refrain to take to arms because they are afraid, one must rather say that they are 'without war' rather than say they are 'in peace.' For peace is not merely a condition without war; it is a virtue that springs from spiritual power." More critical than any other consideration, when it comes to keeping peace and strengthening freedom, is to know the essence of the spiritual power Spinoza describes and then strive to obtain it.

Spiritual power is a capacity within every individual human being. A folk or nationality can possess it only insofar as the individual members possess it. And of what does it consist? It consists of (1) the ability to know thyself to be a spiritual being and thereby able to meet other people without fear for losing one's self even if the other is a different spiritual being, and (2) the doing so without repressing or suppressing the other when he asserts himself, nor does the other need to fear losing himself in the meeting. If I recognize the eternal being within me, I know that it cannot be destroyed by anything that comes from the outside—not by catastrophe or violence—and I know that threats will not set me off track. To the contrary, I can obtain inner peace that can nourish peace in others and remove the spike of their aggression. If we mature in an atmosphere of mutual respect, we can search for solutions to our problems as a community. Is it necessary to believe in order to obtain peace? When I overcome fear and when others realize they have nothing to gain by using threats or violence, then peace can stream from me. If I become nervous or lose my head, I am susceptible to threats, for this cues the worst, most aggressive part of the other. If I am steadfast, the consequent ability of spiritual power appears to sustain freedom, namely respect for others.

Let us consider myself and another in conflict. I must acknowledge that the other has the right to existence, for everyone exists "with the highest natural right," as Spinoza wrote. Therefore it is my duty to be interested in and responsible for the other's legitimate rights. If I know myself as a spiritual being and know that I can find a source of power that streams through spiritual knowledge, I may have the magnanimity to take care of the other's interests. This brings us to the third and most important capacity—living thinking that allows us to find the possibilities and ways when he who has blinders before his eyes sees battle as the only way. The participants in a battle may ask, "Why did the conflict end in open battle?" The answer is often, "Because we did not have the moral imagination that allowed us to see the right solution." If we ask further, "How can the battle end?" the answer is, "When one of us finds the solution to which we can both agree." Mechanistic thinking and lack of imagination are probably the main reasons for the conflicts that rage all over the world still today.

The materialistic way of thinking creates the fear and spiritual rigidity within which irreconcilability appears and war ensues. Alternatively, spiritual thinking can create empowered, peaceful, inner certainty and spiritual mobility. We can see other perspectives and can speak about something that has significance for social life, at the very least within large international circles. Therefore the issue of war and peace is not a question that can be answered by politicians alone, by those who are directly involved in the great decisions. Rather, these decisions belong to everyone, not simply because they affect everyone, but because every human being creates an atmosphere that surrounds him and works upon his environment as a person from whom either a benevolent activity exudes or a nervous, unpeaceful atmosphere. Or where passivity and bluntness enable us to be bricks in the wall and we suffer a result we do not wish.

Peace in the world depends not merely on the actions of leading personalities within two or three power blocks. Peace springs from the spiritual power in every human being. It is essential for everyone to know that he or she is not merely a member of a society or a power block but also an individuality, an independent personality. At the very least it is necessary to overcome thinking collectively, thinking within power blocks. If we believe there are two or three power blocks in the world, we accept that we must be loyal to the one in which we belong. Then limited conflicts are impossible. For, no matter what is happening across the world, I belong to it, I must take side, I must work for peace by contributing so the just side can triumph.

And we feel morally responsible for engaging in the conflicts all over the world, and all peace-loving nations must send peacekeeping troops to the little nations where war is played out by the rest of the world that fights on their territories. For all the peace-loving nations choose sides and send their troops to fight.

No, if one thing is clear concerning idealism it is that no nation can send its sons and daughters to battle in a foreign land. Thinking should be developed out of idealism, from which peace springs. In the battles fought on the soil of small nations, the interests of huge power blocks have infiltrated. Even though they want world peace secured, they are cynical enough to allow small wars to rage for their own interests on other nation's territories. Perhaps *cynical* is not the right word here. Perhaps it is better to use *misfortunate humanity*. Perhaps good will is also present here. For what prevented such an unfortunate war as the Vietnam War from ending is also a result of the materialism that brings about rigid thinking, thinking not able to lead the way to lasting and true social solutions.

Each human being is an individuality, and it is his duty to develop his judgment. No one must blindly align with his government's worldview, it is no one's duty to offer solidarity to a power block that promotes egotistical interests. One of the greatest dangers for peace is the belief in our duty towards international solidarity. That belief arises from corrupted thinking, for such solidarity will make every conflict a thousand times more devastating than it would be without it. Solidarity is an empty phrase. It is used by leaders who, for their own interests, exercise influence over those who do not understand that they are merely bricks in a dishonest game.

War is no longer a legitimate instrument for deciding important disagreements between power blocks. At this point in history, every war will tend toward a World War. The time for nation states is over. Small states allowed themselves be used by the power blocks during the Cold War. They gave up their independence for a false solidarity. By surrendering their own way of life for security, it is now an open question whether they can find and reestablish their independence. Dividing the world into power blocks is a threatening gesture. Therefore the path to true peace begins by dissolving the idea of a state and focusing on individuals who are free of the state's influence, who are working and striving as free people within the economic, political, and religious spheres of life without alliance to any group's interests.

The Power of Moral Education – Geography[1]

by

Christof Goepfer

translated by Ted Warren

If we ask how we can create opportunities for children to form their own moral values, we assume that our pedagogy in Waldorf education can achieve more than merely the transfer of information. We also assume it provides more than support and impulses to the new generation as they take their steps upon the path of knowledge. Must not a school also help children develop a basis for their morality?

These questions set unparalleled expectations of Waldorf teachers, and the teacher's preparations therefore must take on a deeper dimension. It is no longer enough to learn the facts that will be taught; the teacher must somehow deepen meditatively his understanding of the subject. He must become one with the subject over time and experience it inwardly. Then a teacher will notice how the subject is transformed and comes alive, giving his teaching a new power. Upon this starting point the entire consequence of our task as educators is based. We can reflect upon our true goal on many levels:

- The child shall be educated to become a sovereign individual, a human being that can stand on his or her own feet.
- The child shall be creative and retain the ability to learn and change his whole life long.
- We want adults who are not caught in a one-sided world perspective.
- The highest goal is for our children to become sensitive human beings who later have the opportunity to realize spiritual development if they choose to do so.
- We want to educate children to be open for moral ideas, especially at a time when moral values are increasingly being slighted.

The Roots of Morality

In order to provide a basis for morality, it is important to know where morality originates. An ancient proverb states: "Look to the stars and keep your eye on the path." Human morality goes back to "the world of the stars' relationship to the human being and the human being's relationship to the world of the stars." In a lecture series on the origins of morality, Rudolf Steiner taught us that morality is a reflection of our relationship to the hierarchies in the time before birth.[2] Morality belongs to neither social conventions nor unconscious feelings in the soul. By remembering the time before their birth, people will know what is correct and good. Steiner placed great emphasis on the need for teachers to know these spiritual relationships and, in addition to their teaching, to work with spiritual scientific content of this type even if it at first appears foreign. The supersensible world that spiritual science describes is the world morality.[3]

Opportunities at School

If a school can at all work morally invigoratingly, these are intimate processes. We can look first at the curriculum Steiner created based on the spiritual laws found within the process of a child's development. Actual demands such as accelerating intellectual development disturb the spiritual laws in the curriculum and hinder the students in receiving the age-appropriate support they need in each grade.

Secondly, the spiritual laws that work indirectly within the curriculum help support the students. Let us look specifically at these opportunities as Steiner addressed them in relation to the study of geography.[4] Developing an ability to observe correctly as learned in geography lessons will help children direct their soul forces in the direction of the earth. "We provide a certain consolidation of the human being in himself when we teach geography in the proper, observable way. We especially develop the person's interest for the world." Such children relate "more lovingly with their fellow human beings than those who have not learned what it means that everything exists side by side in space.… These things work powerfully on the development of moral forces, and the disregard for geography appears elsewhere as the aversion for loving others, something that is also disregarded in our times."

Thus geography lessons work directly into the human being. "The remittance of good geography lessons is responsible for that which is the great sickness of our times." Steiner did not name precisely what that sickness is, but it is reasonable to assume it is even more prevalent today.

Indirect Effects

The approach in this article is not to cover the particular content in various subjects that directly support the themes of morality or religion, nor to try to grasp the hidden spiritual and moral reasons and the indirect effects that may arise from them. For in lessons in geography—and in all natural scientific subjects—we observe the earth's phenomena not as wasteful products of material processes but inquire as to the meaningful, higher laws that live in them. This can provide the basis for the stability of soul and thereby create responsiveness for moral laws, in other words, bring forth the moral attitudes concerning nature's cosmic laws!

An example from history is the knights of King Arthur. For hundreds of years mankind observed the phenomena of nature—the rhythms of the seasons, the elements of water, air and earth in the rivers' rapids, in waves, wind and weather, in mountain formations and plant growth. The knights not only placed their castles according to such realities. From the cosmic-based laws of nature they created the principles of their social order that they needed for their spiritual tasks in the transition between pre-Christian and Christian times. The stories of King Arthur are pictures of how fulfilled this made them.

The question is whether such an observation of natural forces is possible today. Are we able to bring this sort of study to our pupils? One method may be found in Goethe's article on granite:

> With this attitude I approach you, greatest, most honorable monuments of time. Sitting on a high bare summit and overlooking a wide landscape, I can say to myself: Here you are, resting without intermediary on a ground which reaches down to the deepest recesses of the earth; no more recent layer, no heaped-up, conglomerate debris have laid themselves between you and the firm foundation of the primeval world; you do not walk over a continuous grave as in those fair fruitful valleys; these summits have not brought forth anything living nor have they devoured anything living; they are before all life and above all life. At this moment when the inner attracting and moving forces of the earth have, so to speak, an immediate effect on me, when the influences of the sky hover nearer to me, my mood is raised to higher contemplation of nature and, as the spirit of man brings life to everything, a comparison comes alive in me the loftiness of which I cannot resist. So, lonely, I tell myself, gazing down from this entirely bare summit, and hardly seeing in the distance at its foot a scantily growing bit of moss, so lonely, I say, is the mood of a man who desires to open his soul only to the oldest, first, deepest feelings of truth. Indeed, he can say to himself: here, on the oldest, eternal Altar, built directly on the depth of creation, I offer a sacrifice to the Being of all Beings. I feel the first, firmest beginnings of our existence; I overlook the world, her rockier and her gentler valleys, and her distant, fertile pastures; my soul is lifted above itself and above everything, and longs for the closer sky.[5]

Alone-ness and the enlightened atmosphere Goethe perceives on the granite mountaintop opened his soul for the deepest feelings of truth; the soul longs for "the closer sky." He does not mean the physical sky but one in the world of morality. Goethe speaks of the sacrifice that grips him.

In this direction we see Steiner's understanding of the teacher's role: To awaken in our children true feelings of devotion for nature. In each grade the teacher should have these feelings as a good example for the children. A teacher must work his way into a "geology that is sensitive," an attitude that can be expressed in other subjects as well. Especially in the seventh grade when we learn the types of rocks and observe granite, limestone and slate in relation to life-giving processes on earth, we can provide a good foundation in this direction. Goethe ands his colleagues C.G. Carus and Henrik Steffens formulated fruitful thoughts for this.

Inner Prerequisites

To have such thoughts assumes that one does not view the physical-sensory world as the sole and final reality of creative forces and their beings. Steiner presented vast amounts of information and details for this based on his spiritual-scientific research. His shared knowledge has broadened the traditional studies of science and provided enrichment for everyone, especially those who teach and educate children. This is true even if one does not agree that the supersensible world is the world of morality.

Steiner gave simple exercises to lift the individual beyond the level of sensory observation using thoughts that perceive the world as moral. He stated that if we deepen meditatively the blue sky, we can feel some of the godly mercy, and a feeling of " devotion" can appear. By experiencing the green of the plants, we can gain an understanding of the meaning of the phenomena in the world. The white of the snow reveals some of the quality of being in the substances of the world. Especially class teachers can carefully awaken such feelings in their children. In summary: "In this way we come to something deeper than usual. Nature's outer veil is brushed aside and we enter a world that lies behind the outer veil." [6]

For the highest goal for education—that the child shall be creative and retain the ability to learn and change his whole life long—Steiner also provided guidance: We shall remove all impressions, feelings of soul and time from the home where we grew up. For all of the events in our childhood influence us in a certain, limiting way, in our view the world, an attitude we must overcome, and instead develop an element of freedom.

From this perspective we can now see that geography lessons are key. Children learn about other parts of the world, other life circumstances and ways of thinking. The curriculum for geography is built upon what the children first experience in their own homes. Then the perspective of their home is overlaid with learning about the entire continent they live upon, and then further, other parts of the world. That liberation from one's home is critical for higher development. Spiritual development in earlier times was actually described as being "homeless" as a prerequisite for initiation to the mysteries, in being free to attain a real relationship with a spiritual world. From that perspective we can wonder what the extensive "homelessness" all over the world means for mankind in our times.

The Spiritual View of Nature

Until the Middle Ages, all over Europe, humanity had an instinctive knowledge that living behind natural phenomena, behind the mountains, rivers, clouds, and trees, and so forth, were supersensible beings. Among nature people that knowledge still lives. Modern ethnography has surprising statements about this. Therefore it is meaningful to also include Steiner's presentations. He described in much detail the elemental beings that the wisdom of natural peoples also presents: gnomes, sylphs and others. But Steiner described how certain water, air and warmth phenomena serve as the bodies for higher beings, namely angels, archangels and archai. The hierarchical beings live in the world of morality. That means that in our rivers, seas, waterfalls and sea currents—in all formations within the earth's hydrosphere—angelic beings are manifest. In the great wind formations, within the wandering low pressures, in cyclones, archangelic beings are weaving. (Meteorologists still give human names to high and low pressure areas, and Goethe allows the archangels to call the storms their life element in his "Prologue in Heaven" in Faust.)

Warm air formations that are created over certain areas of the earth are the homes of beings from the archai's hierarchy. What an amazing mental image Steiner gives us. Of course this does not belong in any lessons at school! Together with our students we study the observable elements in the hydro- and atmospheres, and the teacher can know that he speaks indirectly about the bodies of hierarchical beings. Although we can leave these mental images as working hypotheses, we must observe phenomena such as the hole in the ozone layer and other operations in the earth's water and climate with greater seriousness than when we merely think of outer damage. From a spiritual perspective these operations are within the world from which morality appears.

The Inner Construction of the Curriculum in the Upper School

The development of moral capacities through the Waldorf curriculum that we considered at the beginning of this article is especially pertinent for the upper school. While preparing for life our students are guided through all four spheres of the earth's organism: geology, the stream organisms of water and air. And when we teach economic geography and ecology, the subjects are all related to meeting the human being's physical and soul needs. In the final year of school we teach how multi-cultural initiatives appear based on the human Self. In the diversity of cultures, the earth mirrors its ability to carry the Self. Knowledge of the world, the earth and the human being illustrates the constant changes which challenge our students to act ever more responsibly.

ESCAPING

While escaping
What a grand reception
Along the way –

Embedded
in the wind's clothes
feet in the prayers of the sand
that can never say amen
for it must
from the falls to the wings
and beyond –

The sick butterfly
knows once again from the sea –
This stone
With the fly's words
Has been laid in my hands –
Rather than my home
I have the transformation of the world.[7]
                 – Nelly Sachs

IN DER FLUCHT

In der Flucht
Welch grosser Empfang
unterwegs –

Eingehuellt
In der Winde Tuch
Fuesse im Gebet des Sandes
Der niemals Amen sagen kann
Denn er muss
Von der Flosse in den Fluegel
Un weiter –

Der kranke Schmetterling
Weiss bald wieder vom Meer –
Dieser Stein
mit der Inschrift der Fliege
hat sich mir in die Hand gegeben –
An Stelle von Heimat
halte ich die Verwandlungen der Welt.

Endnotes
1. This article was printed originally in *Steinerskolen*, Number 34, March 2004.
2. Steiner, Rudolf. *Man and the World of the Stars*, GA 219, Anthroposophic Press, p. 62.
3. _____. *Theosophy* (GA 9) and *Knowledge of Higher Worlds*, GA 10, both available from SteinerBooks (www.steinerbooks.org).
4. Steiner, Rudolf. *Education for Adolescents* (GA 302), NY: SteinerBooks, 1996.
5. "Granite" by Johann Wolfgang von Goethe, 1784. This essay is available from AWSNA Publications (www.whywaldorfworks.org/publications).
6. Steiner, Rudolf. *The Spiritual Beings in the Heavenly Bodies and in the Kingdom of Nature* (GA 136), lecture 1, NY: Anthroposophic Press, 1967.
7. Nelly Sachs, "In Der Flucht," see *O, the Chimneys: Selected Poems*, translated by Michael Hamburger, New York: Farrar, Straus and Giroux, 1967. Nelly Sachs (1891–1970) was a German poet and dramatist whose Nazi experience transformed her into a poignant spokesperson for the grief and yearnings of her fellow Jews. She was awarded the 1966 Nobel Prize for Literature.

Ethics and the Perspective on Nature

by

Oskar Borgman Hansen

translated by Ted Warren

From observations on the developments over the past four hundred years in natural science, I have defined a path for the renewal of scientific research that includes significant cultural consequences. We all experience as a very serious social problem the cultural divide between science and ethics. These very important aspects of our lives are not in harmony. Many people want scientific research to be subjected to ethical control, and thus, for example, the establishment of Denmark's Ethical Council. Why should research not have its own innate direction such that control from outside is unnecessary? There is a conflicting, dualistic relationship between research and ethics.

Another important dualism, not discussed as often as the one of research and ethics, is the dualism between nature and spirit. The human being is part of the kingdom of nature. We take in nature's substances through food and breath and we release them once they have served our organs. In a certain way we also stand outside of nature: we observe her, we judge her and we make theories about her. Everything that belongs to our comprehension of nature takes place in our inner life, and the process of comprehension has nothing to do with nature. Therefore we often talk about ourselves in relationship to nature rather than as part of nature. This points to a form of duality that is similar to that between research and ethics. Strange as it may be, our distance from the world of nature makes us want to subject her. The goal of science is to make nature subservient to man. This conclusion brings us back to the dualism between research and ethics, for we must ask: Why is it legitimate to control nature?

An old conviction about the goals of studying the natural sciences is that we want to create power over nature. Knowledge is power, not only that one person can have power, but it lies in the essence of knowledge, in its definition, that it brings power. This definition is rooted in the desire for power. We find this desire in the perspective on nature created by the English natural philosopher Francis Bacon (1561–1626). This perspective has defined the very understanding that has brought us to the point where we now have directly contrasting relationships between human beings and nature. People are so antagonistic to nature that they wish to subject it to the point where our exercise of power may well bring about the destruction of nature.

The Finnish-Swedish philosopher Georg Henrik von Wright (1916–2003) published *Science and Reason* in 1986. This book provoked a strong debate before it was soon forgotten. An analytical philosopher his whole life, he began his career in research as a follower of logical positivism, a direction that includes a sharp difference between ethics and knowledge. It argues that we can never reach scientific statements on ethical questions. All reflections are subjective. For example, he who says we should not lie clearly expresses that he does not appreciate lying. From this point of view nothing is considered to work against nature or destroy it. If one says that mankind destroys nature when his agriculture creates erosion, this means, from the logical positivism perspective, that one does not want erosion.

People cannot live in Antarctica and they can barely live on the Sahara. But a desert is merely a landscape among other landscapes. If we achieve a short-term advantage in nature, there is merely one question to be answered: Do the advantages outweigh the disadvantages? No matter what the answer may be, the point of view is always purely subjective and human.

Von Wright wrote that his scientific understanding was shaken when he learned that in America certain industries were forced to pay for cleaning up liquid wastes. He considered this unfair because technology will soon be able to make fish that can live in polluted water and still be edible. There must be something fundamentally wrong with a philosophy that can lead someone to think this way. Yet this way of thinking is not the expression of something out of control, it is a consequence of our last three century's understanding of science. Von Wright tells us to search for reason, but he does not tell us how to find it. Yet he maintains hope that we will find it. This article is an attempt to search for the new reason von Wright longed for, and, when we find it, that reason will guide us to a new relationship with nature.

If we search for something new, it is wise to know what is old, what once was new and considered progressive when first established. One example of this is the mechanical world perspective prevalent in Bacon's time and for which Galileo (1564–1642) became famous. With sharp polemics during the Middle Ages against the understanding of science and nature, these two carried scientific research a step further.

Aristotle (384–322 BC) created a preliminary understanding of science in the fourth pre-Christian century. Yet by the time of the first generation of Christians, there was very little interest in scientific thinking. After centuries of development, by the time of the Middle Ages, a synthesis was found between science and the Christian world perspective. This was done in such way that reconciliation was reached between Aristotle's world perspective and the Jewish-Christian understanding of the relationship between God and the world. Both perspectives entail the conviction that the world was set up pre-conditionally. This pervades the creation stories in the book of Moses, in which God created a good world wherein each phenomenon served the greater whole. For example, God placed the sun in the heavens so there would be light. Further, Aristotle points to an earth created for the reasonable and the good so that everything on the earth has God in its center and as its ultimate goal. It is good that celestial bodies move across the sky. That heavy objects fall is an example that the world is set up for the good.

This was rightfully contested in the seventeenth century. The new goal was to observe how the world really is. No matter how well aligned it was with Christian concepts, Aristotle's perspective explained nothing. It is certainly valuable for people to see with the help of the sun, but would it not be more valuable to have light twenty-four hours a day? When we leave the old explanations behind and begin researching, the laws of nature are discovered. Astronomical laws explain the movement of heavy objects better than the explanation that it is God's plan for creation. Thus the concept of natural laws was established.

Galileo said, "I want to describe, not explain." Galileo understood the explanations of the direction of falling objects to be the "search for their rightful place." When they fall, it is better that they fall than if they do not fall. Instead he wanted to find the mathematical formula that determines everything in their fall.

As theoretical as these statements appear, they are extremely important for understanding the development of science even today. This change of mind has led to modern science and its results on one side and to the estrangement from nature on the other. The latter is largely responsible for our pollution of the environment and dangers related to our relationship with nature. If we can see what the relationship is between the exploitation of nature that includes unwanted, environmental byproducts and dangers on one side and modern scientific research on the other side, we will certainly arrive on the path to the new reason for which we must strive.

Theories are created in human minds. Whenever we think about something, we add something to it that is revealed to us by our senses. For example, our senses reveal to us that things fall. Thinking brings the laws of gravity with mathematical formulas to the experience in our senses as proof. This concept would not have even been conceived in the Middle Ages. Rather, at that time they would have said, "We read the book of nature."

What we add to our theories is nothing more than that which was already there from the beginning. The picture image that we read in "nature's book" is adequate. If you put a book in front of me, the first thing I see are the letters. If the book is published in an unfamiliar language with an alphabet I do not know, then I can see everything but understand nothing. Once I learn the foreign alphabet and language, I can understand. The understanding is something new that I add to the sensory experience, but it has nothing to do with the letters. I now understand only that which was there all along.

As obvious as that may seem, there are few scientific theorists today who will agree. Instead they say that with our theories we are adding something to that which our senses show us, especially through experiments. They do not believe that what we think we are adding was already there. Our senses shall show us the surface, and we do not know what reality hides behind the surface, if indeed there is something hidden there. We must be content with relating to things on the surface. Their essence remains hidden forever. And this shall be true for all areas of being with one exception. If we base our reflections for a moment on Immanuel Kant (1724–1804), who has expressed that the essence of things remains hidden, the exception can be characterized as follows:

With scientific knowledge, we remain outside of the objects and describe merely the outer laws for what we experience on the surface. But human beings are not merely natural beings. They have a consciousness of themselves as morally responsible beings. Nature does not explain the realities of morality. Kant mentions that no one can or wants to refute this statement, for we all know that there are some things that are allowed and some things that are not allowed and, further, that these allowances are not merely according to outer norms but according to individual conscience. That conscience provides, in its reality, the proof that human beings are not merely natural beings but also spiritual beings. Yet we cannot actually grasp mankind's duality as a natural being and a moral being. Nature is such that it locks out morality. In nature the law of cause and effect can explain everything. Morality does not fit into such patterns. Therefore we cannot explain morality from a psychological perspective. You can say that when Kant wrote his works at the end of the eighteenth century, the Godlike realities were driven out of all walks of life and replaced with a scientific way of thinking with morality as the only and last exception.

Perhaps it is easiest to see how the mechanical world perspective falls short when we observe the human being. According to its world perspective scientific psychology asks the following methodological question: As the human being is a part of nature, can we find the laws that allow us to know how people react under certain conditions?

If we know that, we can, for example, design education based on a scientific understanding that allows us to calculate the best conditions to help children develop certain skills. By systematically observing children, we find that the most effective learning process is when the teaching happens for so many minutes or hours and then a break is given. We can also learn that this relationship varies according to the age of the children. The method of obtaining this knowledge is called *experimental psychology*. It is no longer dominant but consequent representatives remain. American psychologist B.F. Skinner (1904–1990) argued this perspective in his much-read book *Beyond Freedom and Dignity*, that entrenched belief in the moral autonomy of the individual ("dignity") hindered the prospect of using scientific methods to modify behavior for the purpose of building a happier and better organized society.

It is important for us to acknowledge the basic questions of this work: How do people react under certain conditions? How do we influence them based on our knowledge of these reactions? Yet, if we have no previous expectations for how to ask such questions, we might ask another question: Which form of education most benefits children? One may consider it simple to say that the last question is the most fundamental question for education. But in order to ask that question, we must have a new understanding of what science is. We must have a science on the child's being, not merely a science of its reaction patterns.

In all of its different manifestations, psychoanalysis has acknowledged that we must differentiate between the surface and the being. On the surface, different people perform actions that appear identical. In the being, one acts from force or convention, the other acts as a free expression of being. The task of psychology is to teach people to be themselves, something they not always are. If one is able to speak that way, which many people can, then one has already broken from the form of science that is connected to the mechanical world view which has been developed since Bacon and Galileo's time. Yet psychoanalysis, in particular from Sigmund Freud's point of view concerning the human being, has not fully broken off consequently. For Freud (1856–1939) it was a reality that no matter what else human beings are, they are beings of nature; i.e., that the nature of human beings unfolds within the needs that are given by the psychological-biological structure. But Freud did not pursue this because it was so obvious to him.

Today we should be able to see the limitations of such a materialistic understanding of the human being. Anyone who understands the human being does so in the power of something that goes beyond, that reaches beyond everything that is based in the biological aspects of human life. To be a good teacher one needs to have an intuitive ability to love. This is where the understanding of what science is plays a role. He who asks only how one might best teach children certain desired skills misses out on asking, more importantly, what might best serve the child and help develop the child's ability to ask the essential questions. When I use the phrase "certain desired skills," we must be clear that I speak of what is desired by society, how the environment wants children to be. Today we witness people asking whether children can meet the demands of college admission and successful careers. To understand is to exercise power, says Bacon. His way of thinking still has followers today, even in regards to the understanding of the human being. To those who say I draw too sharp a line, I would reply that it is necessary in order to clearly define the essential, even when it can be hard to find consequent followers of the sharp opinions.

Today it is common to speak about civil rights. Human rights are something that appear for those who observe human life superficially. As sensory beings we have no human rights. As beings in this world we have rights that our society give us, for example the right to vacation for a certain number of days. Rights are always concrete when considering the human being as a being in the sensory world. In contrast to the actual rights given by society, "human rights" is an idea, something supersensible, something merely thought. But that which is "merely thought" must be in line with the human being. Everyone who is able to think something rationally about the concept of "human rights" must have broken with the mechanical world perspective and thereby has already found some of that new rationality for which von Wright was searching.

The human being is a spiritual being who develops from within that which is independent of the biological laws. Just the fact that we can speak about "human rights" points to this. If we could not admit this, we should refrain from speaking about them, for both belong together. And in addition we must have found a new science to be able to speak that way. What gives us this ability? It is the fact that thinking does not strive for power, but rather for understanding. Thinking carries people beyond the merely subjective to that which we all can understand. We could call it trans-subjective. In the sensory world we are introduced to the outer realities of objects. In thinking we meet their being. We may not believe this because this is a departure from our usual way of thinking, but we live in a certain confidence that we can be understood by other people. How else could we speak with them? Many speak with people to influence them or convince them of something. But they know themselves that it is better to be understood and have their points of view accepted on their own merits rather than having them imposed through authority or indoctrination. Yet it is the trans-subjective in thinking that makes free understanding possible. We can say that love is the core of thinking.

The new science demands that we see again that an idea is a reality. There are good reasons for being expelled from the world of science. In the mechanical sciences the assumption that an idea is a reality no doubt suppressed the first stages of research. But the criticism went too far and the unfortunate result was dualism, which is most clearly defined in Kant's philosophy: there are two worlds and we cannot understand how they relate to each other. We assume that ethics belongs to the human being, that is, in the life of mankind. But we cannot understand how ethics relates to nature. Notice the prejudice in the previous statement. The person who acts ethically is also part of the world. What a person experiences in his thinking belongs either to reality or to nature. The human being is part of nature and we can understand our fellow man by thinking. If the idea shall be seriously reintroduced to our thinking about the human being and the world, there are two conditions that shall be fulfilled: We shall reach totalities and we shall see the idea in a concrete situation. If we fulfill both conditions we reach something fruitful.

The idea of human rights is used with every human being. If we remove one person from it we fail what it is all about. Another idea that plays a large role in our thinking, especially after the fall of communism, is the idea of liberal economy, of the meaning of competition for the economy. This idea is abstract and distant from reality. If it were concrete we would not have regulating fixed prices for agricultural products while limiting production to prevent prices from sinking too low. The idea of liberalism does not fit in reality. We also need to ask if liberalism benefits *everyone*? The idea of human rights includes everyone.

An extension of human rights, if we want our economy to strive for brotherhood, is to remove competition in order to help each other. Agriculture must move in new directions. A new form of land ownership can liberate agriculture from the burden of debt, which in reality is not necessary. For example, if we observe biology, we cannot avoid removing the materialistic explanations whenever they are absolute. An animal's organs are determined by particular functions; all animals are determined by the construction of their limbs for certain actions. The human body, most particularly the human hand, demonstrates that people are free beings. Humans can use their hands to hit or to caress, they can write their signatures on a threatening letter or on a gift certificate. The hand obeys the spirit's instruction. But the human being has not created his own body. While the body is the spirit's expression, there must be an active spirit in nature that has built this body during a long evolution.

As the human is a being that unfolds from within, so are all living organisms. But whereas animals and plants are partially or totally unconscious beings, within the human being a conscious spirit works. There are no complete, mechanistic explanations that plants and animals unfold rhythmically. One can ask humorously whether the chicken or the egg came first; they belong together in a development that stretches through time; they demand a development of man's spiritual efforts to understand the living forces. One must build relationships inside in order to be able to hold the moment that unfolds in time.

Kant stated that biology would never be a science in the context of understanding the mission of living beings. At the same time as Kant made this prediction, Goethe was developing a totally new perspective on living nature. Nature can be understood but requires the development of new organs of understanding. We can understand nature in its totality when we observe the phases of development in the natural kingdoms. Goethe (1749–1832) wanted to develop a science in this direction; we call it Goethean science, and Austrian scientist Rudolf Steiner (1861–1925) developed it further. It has grown into a positive direction of scientific research.

A person receives the answer to the questions he asks. Those who research in nature define the direction of their research and subsequent answers by the questions they ask. The question is: Which light do people who search direct towards reality? If we ask what the point is and how we can gain power over nature, we will place ourselves outside of nature and will never escape the unwelcome consequences of our actions. If we ask how we can support life-giving processes, we will enter paths of thinking that will bring forth cultural renewal within a perspective on life that brings the relationship between social and natural scientific thinking into our daily lives.

The Being of the Internet

by

Sergei Prokofieff

Sub-Nature has to be understood as such.
— Rudolf Steiner, March 1925

The Being of the Internet is esoterically best understood on the basis of Rudolf Steiner's Dornach lecture of May 13, 1921.[1] In this lecture Steiner described how the further development of today's abstract intellect will slowly produce a kind of new nature kingdom. This intellect which is merely of a "shadowlike character" can only function "automatically" and can only comprehend the material as such, and never the etheric and to an even lesser degree the soul world or spirit world. This ghostly nature kingdom will be formed between the mineral and the plant kingdoms and come alive following the reunion of the moon with the earth in the Seventh to Eighth Millennium.

The Imagination of the Spider Web

It is frightening how poignantly Steiner described this spirit world in comparison with the world situation of today:

> And from the earth will well up terrible creations of beings who in their character stand between the mineral kingdom and the plant kingdom as automative beings with super-natural intellect, an immense intellect. When this development takes hold, the earth will be covered, as with a web, a web of terrible spiders, spiders of enormous wisdom, which however, in their organization don't even reach the plant status. Terrible spiders which will interlock with each other, which will imitate in their movements all that which humanity has thought of with their shadowlike intellect that was not inspired by a new imagination, through that which is to come through Spiritual Science. All man's thoughts of this kind, which are unreal, will come alive. The earth will be covered ... with terrible mineral-plant-like spiders, which will link up with empathy but evil intention. And man ... will have to unite with these terrible mineral-plant-like spider creatures.[2]

These spider creatures will be of a distinct ahrimanic character. When one reads these prophetic words of the spiritual scientist today, in an era of world-wide connections via computer and the Internet, one may be disheartened to find how quickly this prophecy has become a reality on earth. It is as if Steiner, with his spiritual gaze, described today's Internet from beyond the threshold, categorically warning humanity that in a not too distant future, with the unification of moon and earth, this whole Internet-computer-web, and in fact everything connected with the development of the artificial intellect, will suddenly come alive and humans "will have to unit his life with these terrible mineral-plant-like spider creatures." If one considers how many people, in particular young people, have become computer addicted and spend most of their time in front of the screen without sufficient will to get away from it, then one can imagine how endlessly greater the dependence on this spider kingdom will be if in the future this whole net comes alive. Mankind will hardly have a chance to disconnect from it. The frightening picture of an insect caught in the net of a huge and ravenous spider, trying in vain to free itself, is an appropriate picture of this future for mankind. And it will be a very special task of white magic to free such people from their bond to these beings.

Created with Intent

In this lecture Steiner also pointed to the fact that there are certain occult circles which are well aware of this approaching danger and who are intent on advancing it by deliberately keeping this secret.

> "There are those [human beings] who are quite consciously allies of the intention to en-web human existence."[3]

If one takes Steiner's words seriously, there can be no doubt that these occult circles, which know of the above mentioned secrets and yet push mankind in this forlorn direction, have also found a suitable name for the internet, the most appropriate instrument to achieve this future, and spread it like a secret code: www = world wide web.

In my opinion these occult circles belong to those secret brotherhoods of the English-speaking West about whose occult-political endeavors Steiner advised us in his lectures during World War I.[4] That does not mean however, that those who have given the Internet its name themselves belong to these occult circles. They usually are more or less figures outside who are being used and do not know about it. This begs the question whether some of the other labels in the world have arisen from the same source e.g. the hotel chain in Germany called "Sorat" (the largest hotel and in the center of Berlin), and the satellite aerials which in the center of the dish display in big red letter the name "SatAn," and the latest computer system in which one finds demonic pictures and words such as the Internet browser "Mozilla" which portrays the head of a red dragon, and so forth.[5] At the end of the lecture Steiner reiterated, as if in anticipation of criticisms from some anthroposophists: "Mankind may close its eyes to such things; they may say: Well, this is reading too much into it. But the signs are really there and the signs should be understood by humanity."[6] And to such signs, which can be seen clearly today and must be understood, in particular by anthroposophists, also belongs the following.

The Number of the Beast

According to the occult teachings of the Kabala all Hebrew letters have a numeric equivalent. Steiner spoke about this in detail in his cycle on the Apocalypse concerning the revelation of the name of the sun demon *Sorat*.[7] On this occasion Steiner pointed out that the numeric equivalent of the letter *W* (Hebrew *waw*) is 6, the number 6. It follows that the occult meaning of "www" is "666," the number of the beast of which the apocalypse says: "Here wisdom itself speaks. Whoever has the ability to think it, let him seek the meaning of the number of the beast. It is the number of Man. And its number is six hundred and sixty-six."[8] The indication of the "number of Man" means that the beast, which is not of human nature, will use something coming from man himself for its attacks against humanity. In my opinion the Internet and everything connected to artificial intelligence are part of this.

In conclusion, the aims of the above mentioned occult circles not only relate to the spiritual en-webbing of humanity but ultimately to the endeavor to put the whole undertaking into the service of Sorat. Because the latter is the prime opponent of the Ego-principle within mankind, the en-webbing of humanity through the artificial intelligence that has come alive will lead ultimately to the loss of the Ego.

Connecting to Sub-Nature

It is clear to see that today's digital industry is being driven exactly in this direction. At present chips are produced as the basis for computers in which predominantly electricity is used as the information carrier or store. However, the next generation of chips is already at the door, chips which use not only electricity but also light as a transmitter. This means that a chip of the same size can contain a thousandfold more information. And this is not by far the pinnacle of development in this field, as there are already large companies in the West which are experimenting with chips that will no longer be based on light but on microbiological elements as information carriers. These new "biological chips" will again increase the capacity for information they can hold compared to "light chips" a thousandfold. Since the biochips are infiltrated with electricity, they are united with sub-nature from the start. Thus the whole development undoubtedly moves closer towards Steiner's imagination of an earth covered and later enlivened by a spider web.

Electronically Compressed

Something similar, although in a different format, happens with a compact disc (CD), digital versatile disc (DVD), or an external hard drive. To understand what this actually means, one has to remember that when the cosmic intelligence guarded by Michael descended from the sun to the earth in order to become human intelligence there,[9] it went through a massive process of compression or contraction. This intelligence, if not seized by Ahriman in the human being, only becomes "naturally" free after death during the expansion of the ether body in the cosmos, i.e., during the process which forms the polarity to its compression. Only a modern schooling path which has the development of living thought as its root can bring about this expansion into the spiritual world already during earthly life and hence ensure a new, conscious connection of mankind with the cosmos and there with Michael himself. The ahrimanic powers serving Sorat work in opposition to this, especially after 1998 (3 x 666).[10] Ahriman—making use of the forces of sub-nature—wants to penetrate the Michaelic intelligence with the artificial intelligence created by him, which includes the digitization of thought. For him this is one of the ways in which he can gain power of earthly intelligence. This started with the fixation of human thoughts through the process of printing and continues now through digitization.

"What does Ahriman intend to gain from Michael through print?" He wants—and you can see that appear everywhere today—to conquer intelligence, that conquest of intelligence which is particularly easy to attain, where conditions are favorable."[11] And Ahriman finds such favorable conditions especially in the world of artificial intelligence and digital industry.

Anthroposophical Material

Thus it is possible to grasp with both hands the process of "compression" of anthroposophical material in an ahrimanic sense. The entire collection of Steiner's works today encompasses nearly 350 volumes; digitally collated on CD-ROM, this still means a fair number of CDs. With the use of the latest DVD technology, all 350 volumes can be compressed onto two or three disks. On a hard disk drive there will be sufficient space left for the artistic legacy. If one has some feeling for a spiritual perspective, one can experience a physical pain simply by thinking about this. At the same time this incredible fixation and compression of spiritual material is achieved by dragging the CD/DVD and computer industry even further into the sub-nature—in contrast to print media which already bears Ahriman's imprint, but because of the way it was originally discovered and to a certain degree it is still connected to the natural world through its mechanical process. There, however, the ahrimanic forces possess extraordinary powers with which they will devise even bigger technical wonders in future than is the case so far.

One must not fall prey to the illusion that it is possible to "redeem" the Internet or CD/DVD in the way Steiner indicated for printing. In the realm of sub-nature the obstacles are far greater. One of the reasons for this is the main condition Steiner gives for the redemption of print: "We have to redeem print through reverent feeling for what lives in Michaelic wisdom."[12] In contrast the Internet or DVD puts everything on the level of purely abstract information that in addition comes in "bytes" (this brings up the picture of Osiris cut into pieces by Set) and thus is spread amongst mankind in a way towards which no "reverent feeling" is possible.

The Delusion of the Duad

If one looks behind the being of the computer on this basis, i.e., to the way information is processed and stored, then one discovers that everything is built on the duad which can endlessly and quantitatively be multiplied through repetition and differing compositions. Steiner called this fundamental principle, which forms the basis for computers worldwide the "delusion of the duad."[13] It also connects directly to that force within humanity that in our time fights most ardently against the Michaelic impulse, which is always linked to the number "three." "It is contained in this new consciousness of mankind the delusion of the duad and it veils the truth of the number three."[14] And then Steiner described how everything that arises out of Michaelic inspiration is always threefold: The Threefold Social Order, the three figures in the Representative of Man, the rhythm of the Foundation Stone Meditation, and so forth. Here the Anthroposophical Society and in particular the School of Spiritual Science have a special task: to consciously oppose the ahrimanic principle of the duad, which has spread worldwide—in particular through computers—with the threefold Michaelic principle as the most important foundation stone for a future spiritual culture and to implement it in all areas of human life and activities.

Ahriman's Incarnation

In the same lecture Steiner spoke further about the duad: "Everything that is active in this illusory conception is the creation of the ahrimanic influence, of that influence which in the future will concentrate in the incarnation of Ahriman of which I have already spoken."[15] It follows that the whole computer and Internet industry is today the most effective way to prepare for the imminent incarnation of Ahriman, or at the least to allow his earthly task to run as smoothly as possible for him. The net of ahrimanic spider beings developing out of the internet around the earth stands right from the beginning in a direct relationship to Ahriman appearing in a physical body and will serve him particularly effectively and offer him extremely favorable potential to work.

Already today one can find on the Internet the most awful and defamatory attacks on Steiner, anthroposophy, Waldorf schools and other institutions connected with anthroposophy. This widespread effect far exceeds that of print. There is no doubt that this will increase in the future, particularly with the posting of the collective works on the Internet and DVD because then all alleged "vulnerable passages" in the collective works will be easily and quickly accessible.

Management of the Computer

What has been said does not mean, however, that one should therefore refrain from using a computer or the Internet. They belong to our civilization and at the same time to the greatest ahrimanic provocations which mankind faces and will have to face increasingly in the future. What is crucial however, as with many similar challenges, which we are faced with in today's civilization, is whether the human being controls the computer and the Internet or they the human being. The latter is the easier when we are inclined not to take what Steiner has communicated seriously, or worse ignore it and because of this not notice what in reality is happening. If the human being wants to maintain his autonomy/authority over the world of the computer, then he has to differentiate between what objectively offers pure technical aid for his work and where he oversteps the mark behind which, at first unnoticeable, the ahrimanic seduction will start to take control. In the latter case, without being aware of it, the human being will increasingly become an instrument for alien purposes and slowly slide into the sub-nature himself.[16]

Reading in the Astral Light

In his lecture of January 13, 1924, Steiner pointed to the most important ahrimanic impulses at that time: everything connected to heredity, all forms of nationalism, mechanical thinking in words and finally our train of writing.[17] The latter in particular can effectively apprehend the human being's ascension to reading in the astral light and through this come close to Michael. Therefore, Steiner mentioned that in certain Rosicrucian schools learning to write was prohibited until the fourteenth or fifteenth year of age so that the form, the mechanism that comes to expression in writing, did not enter the human organism. For the same reason letters are taught in Waldorf schools first through drawing and then writing.

Print with its ahrimanic tendencies was inspired through the subterranean "ahrimanic counter/school" of Michael. "Although a spiritual power has to be recognized in the art of printing, it is the spiritual power which Ahriman set opposite Michael."[18] This ahrimanic tendency finds its continuation, if not indeed its culmination, in today's digital forms of print in order to reach its aim even more effectively: to cut man off from his ability to read in the astral light and thereby encounter Michael in the spiritual world.

The New Imaginations

That the Internet not only stands in polarity to the sphere of Michael in the spiritual world but that it is its ahrimanic counterpart can be seen in the way Steiner described the being of cosmic intelligence: "Intelligence forms the mutual law of conduct amongst the higher hierarchies. What they do and how they interact, how they relate to one another, that is cosmic intelligence."[19] The Internet increasingly takes on a similar function among human beings. Here the attempt is made in purely ahrimanic form to create a worldwide web that connects as many people as possible but in a way that mankind becomes increasingly separated from the cosmos and the hierarchies and thus is bound up in an ahrimanic spider web. The Michaelic intelligence came to earth from the spiritual world in order for man to achieve freedom through insight. The above-mentioned addiction to the computer however, leads to the exact opposite.

Through the continued separation of man from the spiritual world, the "human intellect will become increasingly shadowy."[20] Precisely with the introduction of the computer worldwide this process has been enhanced. To counteract this one has to include the "new imaginations" of Spiritual Science into today's "shadowy concepts and intellectual ideas."[21] However, through imprinting their contents onto DVD, the exact opposite is achieved. As purely intellectual "information" on the World Wide Web, the living imaginations of anthroposophy are being put into an occult prison.

The Exceptionality of the Class Texts

The publication of the class texts (as well as the ritual of other esoteric texts by Steiner) on the Internet can be experienced as particularly tragic. Especially in this respect Steiner differentiated between the contents of the class and his other occult lectures. The latter are given to mankind as thoughts and ideas, and appear therefore right from the beginning as if protected by a sheath. (Thus was Steiner able to agree to general publication after the Christmas Conference.)

Concerning the contents of the class, it is a different matter. Here we have a substance, which comes directly from Michael himself (out of the Michael-School) and therefore contains imaginations in their original form, which demand a totally different handling. Steiner pointed to this character of the class contents as follows: "Therefore it will generally have to be thus, that man gets to know the spiritual world first of all in the form of ideas. This is the way Spiritual Science will be cultivated within the General Anthroposophical Society. However, there will be those who wish to go a step further in the descriptions of the spiritual world, from ideas to expressions which themselves are received from the spiritual world. ... It will be for them that the three classes of the 'school' will be available. There the work will achieve an ever-increasing degree of esotericism. The 'school' will lead the participant into regions of the spiritual world which cannot be revealed through ideas. Here the necessity will arise to find expressions for imagination, inspiration and intuition."[22] Hence the way we treat the class contents has to differ fundamentally from the way we treat Steiner's general lecture contents. He demanded quite clearly a different relationship to the contents of the class than one has to the publication of this lectures.

Dangers and Tasks

During a private conversation Steiner once pointed towards the greatest future danger of anthroposophy—its increasingly intellectualization through which it will be handed to Ahriman, the Master of Death. The posting of Steiner's complete works on the Internet enhances this danger and with it takes a further step towards the intellectualization and cutting up of anthroposophy.

This event has to be countered with an increased and conscious intensification of esoteric work within the School of Spiritual Science as well as meticulous and free from intellectualization study of Steiner's texts. He himself expected this way of working with the texts—not with abstract and increasingly shadowlike intellect, but with the "hearts" which, in the

Michaelic sense "start to have thoughts"[23] and are therefore enabled to reach real imaginations. Only in this way will a place be created within the human being and for future mankind where anthroposophical wisdom is protected from Sorat and the ahrimanic powers serving him. Such care for anthroposophy must be a primary task for all groups within the Anthroposophical Society.

Endnotes:
1. Steiner, Rudolf. *Perspective on Humanity's Development* (out of print).
2. Ibid.
3. Ibid.
4. For example, Rudolf Steiner's *Karma of Untruthfulness*, Vol. 1, New York: Anthroposophic Press (SteinerBooks), 2001.
5. The Bible, New Testament, The Apocolypse of St. John, Chapter 12.3.
6. Op. cit., Steiner. *Perspective*.
7. Steiner, Rudolf. *The Apocolypse of St. John,* New York: Anthroposophic Press (SteinerBooks), 1993.
8. Op. cit., The Bible, Chapters 13 and 18.
9. Steiner, Rudolf. *Karmic Relationships VI*, lecture of July 19, 1924, New York: Anthroposophic Press (SteinerBooks), 1999.
10. Concerning the special relationship of Sorat to the ahrimanic spirits, see Rudolf Steiner's *Three Streams of Evolution of Mankind*, see http://www.kheper.net/topics/Anthroposophy/Steiner-3streams.htm.
11. See above.
12. See above.
13. Steiner, Rudolf. *The Mission of the Archangel Michael, the Revelation of the Secrets of Man's Being* (GA 194), lecture held on November 14, 1919, New York: Anthroposophic Press (SteinerBooks), 1998.
14. Ibid.
15. Ibid.
16. Steiner, Rudolf. *Anthroposophical Leading Thoughts* (GA 26) "From Nature to Sub-Nature," New York: Anthroposophic Press (SteinerBooks), 1998.
17. Steiner, Rudolf. *Mysterien des Mittelalters, Rosenkreuzertim und modernes Einweihungsprinzip* (GA 233a).
18. Op. cit., Steiner. *Karmic Relationships VI*.

19. Steiner, Rudolf. *Karmic Relationships III*, lecture of August 8, 1924, New York: Anthroposophic Press (SteinerBooks), 2002.
20. Op. cit., Steiner. *Perspective*.
21. Ibid.
22. Steiner, Rudolf. *The Constitution of the General Anthroposhical Society and the School of Spiritual Science* (GA 260a), lecture of January 20, 1924.
23. Op. cit., Steiner. *Anthroposophical Leading Thoughts*.

"The Being of the Internet" by Sergei Prokofieff, reprinted with permission from *The Anthroposophical Society in Great Britain Newsletter*, September 2005, vol. 82, no. 4, pp. 2–5.

www.ingramcontent.com/pod-product-compliance
Lightning Source LLC
Chambersburg PA
CBHW080412230426
43662CB00016B/2387